EVOLVE

STUDENT'S BOOK

with Digital Pack

Ben Goldstein and Ceri Jones

T0372782

6A

CAMBRIDGE
UNIVERSITY PRESS

Shaftesbury Road, Cambridge CB2 8EA, United Kingdom

One Liberty Plaza, 20th Floor, New York, NY 10006, USA

477 Williamstown Road, Port Melbourne, VIC 3207, Australia

314–321, 3rd Floor, Plot 3, Splendor Forum, Jasola District Centre, New Delhi – 110025, India

103 Penang Road, #05–06/07, Visioncrest Commercial, Singapore 238467

Cambridge University Press & Assessment is a department of the University of Cambridge.

We share the University's mission to contribute to society through the pursuit of education, learning and research at the highest international levels of excellence.

www.cambridge.org
Information on this title: www.cambridge.org/9781009237598

First published with Digital Pack 2022

20 19 18 17 16 15 14 13 12 11 10 9 8 7 6 5 4 3 2

Printed in Poland by Opolgraf

A catalogue record for this publication is available from the British Library

ISBN 978-1-009-23088-9 Student's Book with eBook
ISBN 978-1-009-23758-1 Student's Book with Digital Pack
ISBN 978-1-009-23759-8 Student's Book with Digital Pack A
ISBN 978-1-009-23760-4 Student's Book with Digital Pack B
ISBN 978-1-108-40909-4 Workbook with Audio
ISBN 978-1-108-40885-1 Workbook with Audio A
ISBN 978-1-108-41196-7 Workbook with Audio B
ISBN 978-1-108-40520-1 Teacher's Edition with Test Generator
ISBN 978-1-108-41077-9 Presentation Plus
ISBN 978-1-108-41206-3 Class Audio CDs
ISBN 978-1-108-40802-8 Video Resource Book with DVD
ISBN 978-1-009-23070-4 Full Contact with Digital Pack

Additional resources for this publication at www.cambridge.org/evolve

ACKNOWLEDGMENTS

The *Evolve* publishers would like to thank the following individuals and institutions who have contributed their time and insights into the development of the course:

Antonio Machuca Montalvo, **Organización The Institute TITUELS**, Veracruz, Mexico; Asli Derin Anaç, **Istanbul Bilgi University**, Turkey; Claudia Piccoli Díaz, **Harmon Hall**, Mexico; Professor Daniel Enrique Hernández Cruz, **Fundación Universitaria Unimonserrate**, Colombia; Daniel Martin, **CELLEP**, Brazil; Daniel Nowatnick, USA; Daniel Valderrama, **Centro Colombo Americano de Bogota**, Colombia; Diego Ribeiro Santos, **Universidade Anhembri Morumbi**, São Paulo, Brazil; Isabela Villas Boas, **Casa Thomas Jefferson**, Brasília, Brazil; Ivanova Monteros, **Universidad Tecnológica Equinoccial**, Ecuador; Lenise Butler, **Laureate Languages**, Mexico; Lillian Dantas; Professor Lizette Antonia Mendoza Huertas, **Fundación Universitaria Unimonserrate**, Colombia; Maria Araceli Hernández Tovar, **Instituto Tecnológico Superior de San Luis Potosí**, Capital, Mexico; Ray Purdey, **ELS Educational Services**; Roberta Freitas, **IBEU**, Rio de Janeiro, Brazil; Rosario Aste Rentería, **Instituto De Emprendedores USIL**, Peru; Verónica Nolivos Arellano, **Centro Ecuatoriano Norteamericano**, Quito, Equador.

To our speaking competition winners, who have contributed their ideas:

Ana Netto, Brazil; Andressa Zanfonatto Slongo, Brazil; Betsi García Alonso, Mexico; Carlos Alfredo Reyes, Honduras; Daniela Estefanía Mota Silva, Mexico; Katherine, Ecuador; Marcelo Piscitelli, Brazil; Renata Lima Cardoso Mendes, Brazil; Stephanie, Honduras; Victoria Rueda Leister Pinto, Brazil.

To our expert speakers, who have contributed their time:
Andrea Mendoza, Audrey Decker, Eric Rodriguez, João Glauber Barbosa, Ryoko Mathes, Susanne Gutermuth.

And special thanks to Wayne Rimmer for writing the Pronunciation sections, and to Laura Patsko for her expert input.

Authors' Acknowledgments

A special thanks to all the editorial team, particularly Dena Daniel, whose patience and professionalism helped make this project a pleasure to work on.

The authors and publishers acknowledge the following sources of copyright material and are grateful for the permissions granted. While every effort has been made, it has not always been possible to identify the sources of all the material used, or to trace all copyright holders. If any omissions are brought to our notice, we will be happy to include the appropriate acknowledgements on reprinting and in the next update to the digital edition, as applicable.

Key: REV = Review, U = Unit.

Text
U5: Project Remote for the text about 'Project Remote'. Reproduced with kind permission of Ryan Means.

Photography
All photographs are sourced from Getty Images.

U1–U6: Tom Merton/Caiaimage; U1: Westend61; wonry/E+; Javier Pierini/The Image Bank/Getty Images Plus; Alliya23/iStock/Getty Images Plus; Charly Triballeau/Stringer/AFP; TPG/Getty Images Entertainment; Bloomberg; baloon111/iStock/Getty Images Plus; Leren Lu/The Image Bank/Getty Images Plus; Dennis Bernardo/EyeEm; olgalngs/iStock Editorial/Getty Images Plus; U2: Image Source; Plume Creative/DigitalVision; Juanmonino/E+; Lane Oatey/Blue Jean Images; Fancy/Veer/Corbis; Mint Images RF; Westend61; Ian Ross Pettigrew; Magone/iStock/Getty Images Plus; undefined undefined/iStock/Getty Images Plus; Viorika/E+; BraunS/E+; Yevgen Romanenko/Moment; NYS444/iStock/Getty Images Plus; numbeos/E+; U3: Cliff Philipiah/Photolibrary/Getty Images Plus; avid_creative/E+; Westend61; Delmaine Donson/E+; simonkr/iStock/Getty Images Plus; bowdenimages/iStock/Getty Images Plus; Fiona McAllister Photography/Moment; U4: thanes satsutthi; Power And Syred/Science Photo Library/Getty Images Plus; Steve Gschmeissner/Science Photo Library/Getty Images Plus; Steve Gschmeissner/Science Photo Library/Getty Images Plus; JoSon/DigitalVision; zazamaza/iStock/Getty Images Plus; Micro Discovery/Corbis Documentary/Getty Images Plus; Clouds Hill Imaging Ltd./Corbis NX/Getty Images Plus; ER Productions Limited/DigitalVision; ArminStautBerlin/iStock/Getty Images Plus; Mariia Romanchuk/EyeEm; Dimitri Otis/DigitalVision; Danielle Hogan/FOAP; Blend Images - JGI; Jena Ardell/Moment; d3sign/Moment; U5: Seth K. Hughes/Image Source; Evgeny Tchebotarev/500px Prime; Cavan Images; DaniloAndjus/E+; Hero Images; AndreyPopov/iStock/Getty Images Plus; U6: skynesher/E+; Oliver Furrer/Photographer's Choice/Getty Images Plus; Bill Heinsohn/Photographer's Choice/Getty Images Plus; Graiki/Moment; Robert Riger/Getty Images Sport; HEX; JohnnyGreig/E+; Maskot; Brand X Pictures/Stockbyte/Getty Images Plus; Ilya Rumyantsev/iStock/Getty Images Plus; kahramaninsan/E+; Frank Gaglione/Photolibrary/Getty Images Plus; REV2: migin/iStock/Getty Images Plus.

The following photographs are sourced from other libraries/sources.

U1: RM Studio/Shutterstock; Courtesy of Consequential Robotics; U3: Paul Christian Gordon/Alamy Stock Photo; U4: thanes satsutthi/Shutterstock; U5: © Automattic Inc. Reproduced with kind permission of Matt Mullenweg; Courtesy of Ryan Means.

Front cover photography by Hans Neleman/The Image Bank/Getty Images Plus/Getty Images.

Illustration
U2: Pete Ellis (D'Avila Illustration); U3: Gavin Reece (New Division); REV1: Robert Filip (Good Illustration).

Audio production by CityVox, New York.

EVOLVE

SPEAKING MATTERS

EVOLVE is a six-level American English course for adults and young adults, taking students from beginner to advanced levels (CEFR A1 to C1).

Drawing on insights from language teaching experts and real students, EVOLVE is a general English course that gets students speaking with confidence.

This student-centered course covers all skills and focuses on the most effective and efficient ways to make progress in English.

Confidence in teaching.
Joy in learning.

Better Learning WITH EVOLVE

Better Learning is our simple approach where insights we've gained from research have helped shape content that drives results. Language evolves, and so does the way we learn. This course takes a flexible, student-centered approach to English language teaching.

EVOLVE
STUDENT'S BOOK
Ben Goldstein and Ceri Jones
6

Meet our expert speakers

Our expert speakers are highly proficient non-native speakers of English living and working in the New York City area.

Videos and ideas from our expert speakers feature throughout the Student's Book for you to respond and react to.

Scan the QR codes below to listen to their stories.

Andrea Mendoza
from Colombia
Financial analyst

Eric Rodriguez
from Ecuador
Graphic designer

Ryoko Mathes
from Japan
Academic advisor

Audrey Decker
from France
Co-founder of a non-profit organization

João Glauber Barbosa
from Brazil
Works in finance for an insurance company.

Susanne Gutermuth
from Germany
Real estate agent

INSIGHT

Research shows that achievable speaking role models can be a powerful motivator.

CONTENT

Bite-sized videos feature expert speakers talking about topics in the Student's Book.

RESULT

Students are motivated to speak and share their ideas.

Student-generated content

EVOLVE is the first course of its kind to feature real student-generated content. We spoke to more than 2,000 students from all over the world about the topics they would like to discuss in English and in what situations they would like to be able to speak more confidently. Their ideas are included throughout the Student's Book.

"It's important to provide learners with interesting or stimulating topics."

Teacher, Mexico (Global Teacher Survey, 2017)

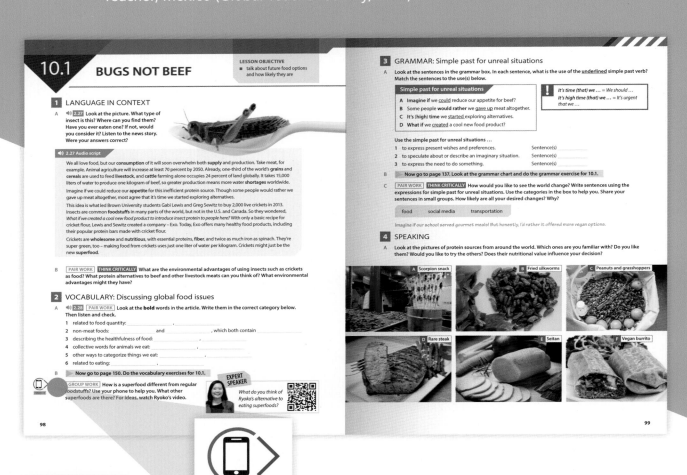

Find it

INSIGHT

Research with hundreds of teachers and students across the globe revealed a desire to expand the classroom and bring the real world in.

CONTENT

Find it are smartphone activities that allow students to bring live content into the class and personalize the learning experience with research and group activities.

RESULT

Students engage in the lesson because it is meaningful to them.

Designed for success

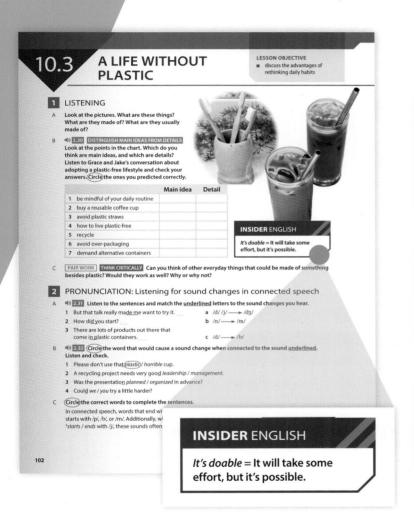

Pronunciation

INSIGHT

Research shows that only certain aspects of pronunciation actually affect comprehensibility and inhibit communication.

CONTENT

EVOLVE focuses on the aspects of pronunciation that most affect communication.

RESULT

Students understand more when listening and can be clearly understood when they speak.

Insider English

INSIGHT

Even in a short exchange, idiomatic language can inhibit understanding.

CONTENT

Insider English focuses on the informal language and colloquial expressions frequently found in everyday situations.

RESULT

Students are confident in the real world.

10.4 WHAT'S YOURS IS MINE

LESSON OBJECTIVE
- write a summary of a discussion about the new economy

1 READING

A Look at the picture of people using a ride-share service. Is this an example of the *gig economy* or the *sharing economy*? What's the difference? You can use your phone to help you. What's your opinion of these new economic models? Why?

B **PREDICT CONTENT** Look at the key words related to the discussion thread below. Which do you think will be used to defend new economic models and which to criticize them? Read the thread and check your answers.

| unfair competition | human-scale commerce | minimum wage |

THE NEW ECONOMY: HAVE YOUR SAY!

Who are the real winners and losers in the gig economy? Is a sharing economy model any better? What do you think?

A
Kevin
When you read about the gig economy, it seems great for everybody, but let me tell you, there are losers in this story. Like taxi drivers. In some countries, it's very expensive to obtain a license – it's an investment. And once you get one, that's your job for life. Then ride-share companies come along, and because of the increased competition, they take away the taxi drivers' livelihood. It's unfair competition because it doesn't cost the other drivers much at all.

B
Amanda
It's time that an economy based on everyone having regular, long-term jobs was challenged. The gig economy is all about on-demand services. Conditions might be more precarious for the worker – job security, insurance, benefits, etc., but we have to get used to that. It's the way the world is going.

C
Abdul
What I like about the sharing economy is that it's a human-scale version of commerce, where you often meet the person who you're doing business with. Take Airbnb. That's a whole lot better than staying in an anonymous hotel somewhere. It's much more personal, and you get better service because of it.

D
Daniel
The sharing economy is nothing new. Just look at libraries. We're just extending that model into the high-tech world. It's inevitable, like economic evolution. There's nothing we can do to stop it, so we might as well go with it.

E
Laura
The "gig economy" business model revolves around tech companies that view legal regulations as outdated or irrelevant. They don't want to follow the rules, so they come up with a way to get around them. They still make money, but the people actually doing the work are NOT better off. In fact, the workers are all independent contractors rather than employees, so they don't get vacations or a minimum wage or sick pay or help saving for retirement. And what's worse, they can be fired without warning or explanation, so they can't even complain!

F
Carolina
At first glance, I really liked the idea of opening up the economy. It's great for us customers, but I think a lot of people actually lose out. I mean, look at streaming music services. We save by not having to download music, but how much money do the musicians make once all the middlemen take their cut? And the food delivery apps! They take such a large cut that many restaurants can't afford to use them, so they lose customers they used to have. People need to understand that these cool new companies could be destroying small neighborhood businesses.

G
Sven
Not so fast! In many places the gig economy has really benefited people, like places where there are no taxis, for example. Now people can use a ride service. How is that a bad thing? People can make extra money and learn new skills. I read that Uber offers English courses to their drivers because they know that it'll help them in their work.

C **PAIR WORK** **EVALUATE INFORMATION** Put a check (✓) for the contributors in favor of the new economic models and an X (✗) for those against them. Highlight the main idea in each comment.

D **GROUP WORK** **THINK CRITICALLY** Which of the opinions in the discussion thread do you agree with? Why? What could be the long-term effects of these new economic models?

104

2 WRITING

A Read the summary of the discussion thread. Does it focus on arguments for or against new economic models?

The gig economy and sharing economy raise many different issues and opinions. The topic is **not at all** a simple one, but two clear arguments in favor of new economic models emerge from the discussion thread: freedom of choice and flexibility.
Gig and sharing economy practices liberate people from the rigidity of a traditional working model, **so** it is beneficial to society. **In terms of** customers, they can have whatever they want when they want it – music, a place to stay, food delivery, a ride to the airport. **And for** workers, they are their own bosses, free to set their own hours and determine their income by working as much as they want. **In a nutshell**, the freedom and flexibility offered by these new ways of working make it beneficial to everyone.
Though **probably true** that the gig/sharing economy is here to stay, **even if** we don't like it, the freedom and flexibility it offers has won it many champions.

B **USE APPROPRIATE REGISTER** Look at the **bold** expressions in the summary and their synonyms in the box below. Which set is more formal? Which expressions from the box could substitute for each expression in the summary?

by no means	in brief	in this respect
it would seem	regarding	regardless of whether
with respect to		

REGISTER CHECK

When writing a summary, establish up front that the opinions you're writing about are not your own and then write from that perspective. This avoids the constant repetition of phrases like *According to …* and *As stated by …* .

WRITE IT

C **PLAN** You're going to write a formal summary of the negative viewpoints expressed in the discussion thread. With a partner, look at the main ideas you identified in exercise 1C. What themes could you focus on in your summary?

D **PAIR WORK** Examine the structure of the summary of positive viewpoints in exercise 2A and discuss the questions.
- What is the role of each paragraph?
- How many points are presented in the body (middle) paragraph?

E **PAIR WORK** Work together to write your summary in 150–200 words. Use formal expressions like those in exercise 2B.

F **GROUP WORK** Share your summary with another pair of students and offer feedback. Is the register definitely more formal than the comments in the thread? Did they present all the main points? Did you organize your summaries around the same or different themes?

105

Register check

INSIGHT

Teachers report that their students often struggle to master the differences between written and spoken English.

CONTENT

Register check draws on research into the Cambridge English Corpus and highlights potential problem areas for learners.

RESULT

Students transition confidently between written and spoken English and recognize different levels of formality as well as when to use them appropriately.

> "The presentation is very clear, and there are plenty of opportunities for student practice and production."

Jason Williams, Teacher, Notre Dame Seishin University, Japan

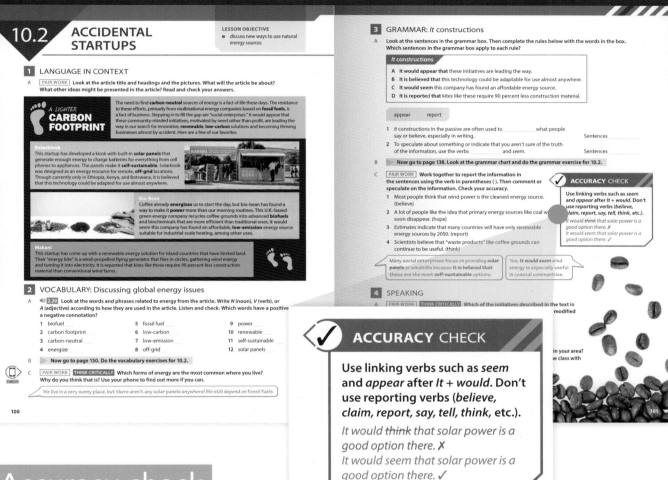

Accuracy check

INSIGHT

Some common errors can become fossilized if not addressed early on in the learning process.

CONTENT

Accuracy check highlights common learner errors (based on unique research into the Cambridge Learner Corpus) and can be used for self-editing.

RESULT

Students avoid common errors in their written and spoken English.

You spoke. We listened.

Students told us that speaking is the most important skill for them to master, while teachers told us that finding speaking activities that engage their students and work in the classroom can be challenging.

That's why EVOLVE has a whole lesson dedicated to speaking: Lesson 5, *Time to speak*.

Time to speak

INSIGHT

Speaking ability is how students most commonly measure their own progress but is also the area where they feel most insecure. To be able to fully exploit speaking opportunities in the classroom, students need a safe speaking environment where they can feel confident, supported, and able to experiment with language.

CONTENT

Time to speak is a unique lesson dedicated to developing speaking skills and is based around immersive tasks that involve information sharing and decision making.

RESULT

Time to speak lessons create a buzz in the classroom where speaking can really thrive, evolve, and take off, resulting in more confident speakers of English.

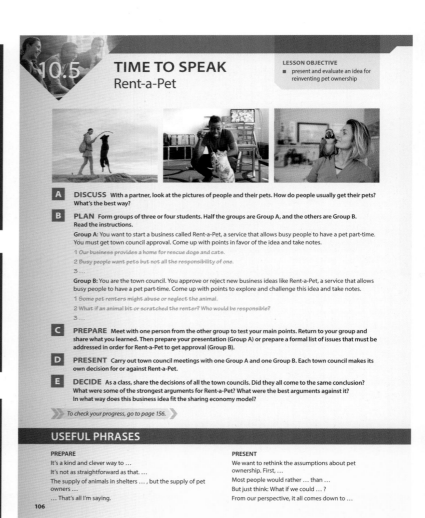

10.5

TIME TO SPEAK
Rent-a-Pet

LESSON OBJECTIVE
- present and evaluate an idea for reinventing pet ownership

A **DISCUSS** With a partner, look at the pictures of people and their pets. How do people usually get their pets? What's the best way?

B **PLAN** Form groups of three or four students. Half the groups are Group A, and the others are Group B. Read the instructions.

Group A: You want to start a business called Rent-a-Pet, a service that allows busy people to have a pet part-time. You must get town council approval. Come up with points in favor of the idea and take notes.
1 Our business provides a home for rescue dogs and cats.
2 Busy people want pets but not all the responsibility of one.
3 …

Group B: You are the town council. You approve or reject new business ideas like Rent-a-Pet, a service that allows busy people to have a pet part-time. Come up with points to explore and challenge this idea and take notes.
1 Some pet renters might abuse or neglect the animal.
2 What if an animal bit or scratched the renter? Who would be responsible?
3 …

C **PREPARE** Meet with one person from the other group to test your main points. Return to your group and share what you learned. Then prepare your presentation (Group A) or prepare a formal list of issues that must be addressed in order for Rent-a-Pet to get approval (Group B).

D **PRESENT** Carry out town council meetings with one Group A and one Group B. Each town council makes its own decision for or against Rent-a-Pet.

E **DECIDE** As a class, share the decisions of all the town councils. Did they all come to the same conclusion? What were some of the strongest arguments for Rent-a-Pet? What were the best arguments against it? In what way does this business idea fit the sharing economy model?

> To check your progress, go to page 156.

USEFUL PHRASES

PREPARE
It's a kind and clever way to …
It's not as straightforward as that. …
The supply of animals in shelters … , but the supply of pet owners …
… That's all I'm saying.

PRESENT
We want to rethink the assumptions about pet ownership. First, …
Most people would rather … than …
But just think: What if we could … ?
From our perspective, it all comes down to …

106

Experience Better Learning with EVOLVE: a course that helps both teachers and students on every step of the language learning journey.

Speaking matters. Find out more about creating safe speaking environments in the classroom.

EVOLVE unit structure

Unit opening page

Each unit opening page activates prior knowledge and vocabulary and immediately gets students speaking.

Lessons 1 and 2

These lessons present and practice the unit vocabulary and grammar in context, helping students discover language rules for themselves. Students then have the opportunity to use this language in well-scaffolded, personalized speaking tasks.

Lesson 3

This lesson is built around an off-the-page dialogue that practices listening skills. It also models and contextualizes useful speaking skills. The final speaking task draws on the language and strategies from the lesson.

Lesson 4

This is a skills lesson based around an engaging reading. Each lesson asks students to think critically and ends with a practical writing task.

Lesson 5

Time to speak is an entire lesson dedicated to developing speaking skills. Students work on collaborative, immersive tasks, which involve information sharing and decision making.

CONTENTS

	Learning objectives	Grammar	Vocabulary	Pronunciation
Unit 1 **Robot revolution**	■ Discuss the potential uses of robots in everyday life ■ Talk about developments in artificial intelligence ■ Acknowledge arguments and propose counterarguments ■ Write an essay about AI in our homes ■ Present a proposal for a robot helper	■ Commenting adverbs with future forms ■ Future perfect and future continuous	■ Using adverbs to add detail ■ Talking about developments in technology	■ Listening for contrastive stress ■ Saying expressions to show a counterargument
Unit 2 **The labels we live by**	■ Discuss assumptions about behavior ■ Talk about assumptions related to age ■ Compare and discuss similar experiences ■ Write a report based on graphs ■ Conduct a survey about consumerism and labels	■ Uses of *will* ■ Uses of *would*	■ Describing personality ■ Using three-word phrasal verbs	■ Listening for the intonation on interactional phrases ■ Saying stressed syllables beginning with /p/, /k/, /t/
Unit 3 **In hindsight**	■ Discuss past actions and their present results ■ React to past situations ■ Describe a negative experience; offer sympathy and reassurance ■ Write a short story based on a set of facts ■ Discuss and present an alternate history	■ Variations on past unreal conditionals ■ Commenting on the past	■ Thought processes ■ Describing emotional reactions	■ Listening for weak forms in complex verb phrases ■ Using intonation to show emphasis
Review 1 (Review of Units 1–3)				
Unit 4 **Close up**	■ Discuss the value of changing perspective ■ Talk about how eyes function in humans and animals ■ Discuss problems caused by staring at screens ■ Write a personal profile statement for a résumé ■ Create and present an action plan for a project	■ Quantifiers and prepositions in relative clauses ■ Noun clauses with question words	■ Describing things ■ Eye idioms and metaphors	■ Listening for /t/ between vowels ■ Saying the stressed syllable in related words
Unit 5 **Remote**	■ Discuss traveling to remote places ■ Comment on loneliness and working in remote places ■ Discuss cause and effect ■ Write a company profile ■ Prepare and present a case for working remotely	■ Participle phrases in initial position ■ Reduced relative clauses	■ Describing remote places ■ Talking about influences	■ Listening for linking between words ■ Saying tense and lax vowels
Unit 6 **Surprise, surprise**	■ Discuss shocks and surprises ■ Talk about great upsets in sports and other contexts ■ Discuss the differences between local and global brands ■ Write a paragraph drawing from multiple sources ■ Prepare a surprise for somebody	■ Clefts ■ Question words with *-ever*	■ Using adverbs to add attitude ■ Using the prefixes *under-* and *over-*	■ Listening for the pronunciation of foreign words and phrases ■ Saying clefts
Review 2 (Review of Units 4–6)				
Grammar charts and practice, pages 129–134 Vocabulary exercises, pages 141–146				

Listening	Speaking skills	Reading	Writing	Speaking
I get what you're saying … ■ A conversation about the innovations found in a new app	■ Acknowledge arguments and propose counterarguments	**Robotics to the rescue** ■ An article about robots and humans working together	**An essay** ■ Introduce examples ■ Organize ideas	■ Talk about the tasks best suited to robots ■ Discuss what things you would like AI to do in the future ■ Offer and support your opinion ■ Discuss interesting examples of AI **Time to speak** ■ Present a proposal for a robot helper to address the needs of a particular job
Same here! ■ A conversation about how speaking another language changes the way you interact with the world	■ Discuss similar experiences	**Read the label** ■ An article about product labeling on healthy food products	**A report based on statistics and graphs** ■ Refer to data in graphs ■ Use language for presenting statistical information	■ Talk about common types of social media users ■ Talk about the right age to do different activities ■ Discuss your experience with language learning ■ Draw conclusions about consumer trends based on statistics **Time to speak** ■ Do a survey about the importance of labels on shopping behavior; present your results
A complete disaster! ■ Two conversations about the same story	■ Describe bad experiences ■ Offer sympathy and reassurance	**Too good to be true** ■ News stories about unlikely events	**An anecdote about a strange coincidence** ■ Create cohesion with *both*, *each*, *neither*, etc.	■ Talk about different possibilities for events in the past ■ Discuss how you might handle different problems ■ Create and share the backstory leading up to a bad experience ■ Discuss and question whether a story is believable **Time to speak** ■ Talk about how changing one past event could affect the world today
Look away! ■ A presentation about the effects of screen time on our eyes	■ Clarify a problem	**Attention to detail** ■ A quiz that reveals if you're a big-picture thinker or tend to focus on details	**A personal profile** ■ Use initial descriptive prepositional phrases for concise writing	■ Talk about the esthetics of close-up imagery ■ React to images of animals' eyes ■ Discuss what problems can occur because of excessive screen time ■ Discuss a personal profile statement; offer suggestions for others **Time to speak** ■ Create and present an action plan that involves both big-picture and detail-oriented tasks
Working from home ■ A presentation about current trends in working from home	■ Signal causes and effects	**Remote success story** ■ A news feature story about a business whose employees work virtually	**A profile** ■ Use participle phrases to connect ideas	■ Discuss where and how you seek solitude ■ Discuss the degree of solitude of different jobs ■ Present and discuss ideas about the pros and cons of current topics ■ Discuss the chances of success for different companies to operate virtually **Time to speak** ■ Make a case for working remotely
A surprising comeback ■ A news feature and interview about business revivals	■ Add emphasis	**Jump scare** ■ Different perspectives on being scared	**Summary of a text** ■ Paraphrase without repetition	■ Talk about reactions to surprises ■ Describe famous upsets ■ Compare local and global industries where you live ■ Write short summaries on articles about fear **Time to speak** ■ Plan a surprise for people based on interviews about their interests

UNIT OBJECTIVES

- discuss the potential uses of robots in everyday life
- talk about developments in artificial intelligence
- acknowledge arguments and propose counterarguments
- write an essay about AI in our homes
- present a proposal for a robot helper

START SPEAKING

A   **Look at the picture. What does it suggest about the future? Do you think it's a realistic vision of the future? Why or why not?**

B   **In what ways do you think technology will change our lives in the future? What kinds of things (wearable technology, personal robots, AI, etc.) do you imagine we'll have in the next 20 years? The next 40 years? In 100 years?**

C   **What kinds of robots do we already use? Do you think robots are a positive invention in general? Why or why not? For ideas, watch Eric's video.**

EXPERT SPEAKER

What examples can you think of to support Eric's argument and to counter it?

THE ROBOT TOUCH

1 LANGUAGE IN CONTEXT

A 🔊 **1.02** **PAIR WORK** **THINK CRITICALLY** What does the robot in the ad look like? What, and who, do you think it's for? What can it do? What can it probably <u>not</u> do? Listen to the infomercial and check your answers.

🔊 **1.02 Audio script**

The MiRo robot may look like a toy, but it is far from it. MiRo is a sophisticated piece of robotic engineering, and it is about to **radically** change the field of home health care.

Though still under development, MiRo will **ultimately** be part of a complex system of sensors and communication networks that will **demonstrably** improve the quality of life for elderly people. MiRo robots will live with their owners 24/7, learn their routines, and monitor their movements, which should **drastically** reduce accidents in the home. They will be able to talk to their owners, as well – reminding them to take their medicine and helping them manage appointments and remember visitors' names. And if there's a medical emergency, MiRo will be able to call for help immediately.

Home health care alternatives are **inevitably** going to become a necessity for countries like Japan and the United States, which are facing the challenge of caring for a **progressively** aging population. Social services will certainly not be able to offer human care and companionship for everyone. Although robot companions are bound to be met with resistance initially, robots like MiRo will **undoubtedly** ease the burden on overstretched social services. The greater benefit, however, will be to the elderly people they serve, who often suffer from loneliness and isolation.

MiRo could **feasibly** revolutionize elder care, making the lives of our senior citizens easier, safer, and far more enjoyable.

INTRODUCING

MiRo!

<u>CLICK HERE</u>
TO ORDER YOURS TODAY!

Courtesy of Consequential Robotics

2 VOCABULARY: Using adverbs to add detail

A 🔊 **1.03** Look at the **bold** adverbs in the script. Which refer to the way something is done (manner)? Which ones are a comment on the action by the speaker (commenting)? Make a chart like the one below and put them in the correct category. Add the other adverbs from the box below. Then listen and check.

comprehensively	dramatically	gradually	increasingly
markedly	potentially	unquestionably	

Adverbs of manner	Commenting adverbs
radically	ultimately

B ▶ Now go to page 141. Do the vocabulary exercises for 1.1.

C **PAIR WORK** **THINK CRITICALLY** Apart from the elderly, who might benefit from having a robot companion? Why? What problems could it solve? What problems might it create?

3 GRAMMAR: Commenting adverbs with future forms

A Read the sentences in the grammar box. (Circle) the correct options to complete the rules.

> **Commenting adverbs with future forms**
>
> MiRo **will undoubtedly ease** the burden on overstretched social services.
>
> Home health care alternatives **are inevitably going to** become a necessity.
>
> Social services **will certainly not be able to** offer human companionship for everyone.

1 Adverbs of manner can be placed in different positions depending on what they modify. Commenting adverbs, when used with future forms, are usually placed …
   - ¹**before** / **after** the modal verb *will*.
   - ²**before** / **after** negative words such as *not* and *never*, or negative contractions such as *won't* and *aren't*.
   - ³**before** / **after** the verb *be* in the phrases *be going to*, *be about to*, and *be bound to*.

B ▶ Now go to page 129. Look at the grammar chart and do the grammar exercise for 1.1.

C PAIR WORK Look at the commenting adverbs in the box below. Use a dictionary or your phone to look up ones you don't know. Then add commenting adverbs to the sentences so that they reflect your opinion. Compare with your partner.

certainly	clearly	eventually	evidently
inevitably	surely	undoubtedly	unfortunately

1 This century will become the age of the robot.
2 Robots are going to change the way we live over the next few decades.
3 Robots will never be able to replace the human touch.
4 Robots are bound to take over for humans in a lot of different areas.
5 The robotics industry is about to make life a lot easier for all of us.

4 SPEAKING

A GROUP WORK THINK CRITICALLY Imagine a robot assistant for the following jobs. What tasks do you think it could feasibly take on? Would it do those tasks better, worse, or as well as a human? What tasks would the human still have to do? Use commenting adverbs to make your attitudes clearer.
   - a clerk in a hotel
   - a nurse in a hospital
   - a teacher in a kindergarten

> As a hotel clerk, a robot **will undoubtedly be** more accurate than a human. It might even be friendlier!

B As a class, share the most interesting uses for a robot assistant that your group came up with. Then discuss whether robot assistants are inevitable. Give reasons to support your opinion.

1.2 THE WONDERFUL WORLD OF AI

1 LANGUAGE IN CONTEXT

A How would you define *artificial intelligence*? Does the idea scare you, worry you, or excite you? Why or why not?

B 🔊 **1.04** Listen to part of a podcast interview in which a tech industry reporter talks about developments in AI. How will AI be used in the near future? How does the host feel about these uses?

> 🔊 **1.04 Audio script**
>
> **Reporter** Industry experts predict that, by the end of the next decade, **chatbots** will have replaced humans in all customer service call centers, but you won't even know you're talking to one. **Computer-generated speech** will have improved so much that chatbots will sound just like humans.
>
> **Host** We'll be having conversations with computers and not even know it? Impressive.
>
> **Reporter** Plus, researchers are developing an app to help blind people "see." It will use the camera on their smartphone to capture the area around them. Then, using a combination of **image-recognition** software and **speech to text**, the app will convert the images into speech. Developers are integrating **facial recognition**, too, so the app can announce when a friend is approaching. They have a **working prototype** now, and they're pretty confident they will have developed a **beta version** for testing by the end of next year!
>
> **Host** What a great use of technology! What other developments can we expect to see soon?
>
> **Reporter** Facial-recognition glasses – they'll be linked to police databases to help pick out suspects in a crowd.
>
> **Host** Really? I'm not sure how I feel about that one.

C PAIR WORK THINK CRITICALLY Why does the host feel nervous about the police using facial-recognition glasses? What are some other possible uses for that technology? What pros and cons can you think of?

2 VOCABULARY: Talking about developments in technology

FIND IT

A 🔊 **1.05** PAIR WORK Look at the technology terms in the box. Write them in the chart for all the things they are associated with. Use a dictionary or your phone to help you. Listen and check.

artificial intelligence (AI)	beta version	chatbot	facial recognition
computer-generated speech	computer translation	image recognition	operating system (OS)
virtual assistant	voice activation	voice recognition	working prototype
text to speech / speech to text			

Home computers	Smartphones	Airport security	App development	Social media
OS	chatbot	facial recognition		

B PAIR WORK Which item from the box above is not yet commonly used? How long do you think it will be until it is part of daily life?

C ▶ Now go to page 141. Do the vocabulary exercises for 1.2.

3 GRAMMAR: Future perfect and future continuous

A Read the sentences in the grammar box. (Circle) the correct options to complete the rules.

> **Future perfect and future continuous**
>
> By the end of the next decade, chatbots **will have replaced** humans in call centers.
> We**'ll be having** conversations with computers and not even know it?

1 Use the future perfect and the future continuous to …
   a describe situations in the future.
   b make suggestions for things to do in the future.

2 Use *will* + *have* + past participle (future perfect) to talk about …
   a actions that will be in progress at a given time in the future.
   b actions that will be completed before a given time in the future.

3 Use *will* + *be* + verb + *-ing* (future continuous) to talk about …
   a actions that will be in progress at a given time in the future.
   b actions that will be completed before a given time in the future.

B ▶ Now go to page 129. Look at the grammar chart and do the grammar exercise for 1.2.

C PAIR WORK You are going away this weekend to an unfamiliar location. A friend asks you a lot of questions about your trip. Use the prompts to write the questions in either the future perfect or the future continuous, and check your accuracy. Compare with a partner.

1 a How / travel / there ?
   How will you be traveling there?
   b Who / meet / there ?
   c What activities / do ?

2 a By the time the weekend is over, who / speak to ?
   b What / see ?
   c What / do ?

> ✓ **ACCURACY** CHECK
>
> **Remember not to change the form of *be* in future continuous.**
>
> *It'll ~~is~~ raining by the time we get there.* ✗
> *It'll be raining by the time we get there.* ✓

D PAIR WORK Answer the questions in exercise 3C and create a story about your weekend trip to tell your partner. Share your stories with another pair of students.

4 SPEAKING

A GROUP WORK Make a list of ten machines and gadgets you have in your home right now. How does each one help you or make life easier? Which of them do you think you'll still be using ten years from now? Will you be operating them, or will they depend on AI? For ideas, watch Eric's video.

EXPERT SPEAKER

How similar are your predictions to Eric's?

B What ordinary tasks or common devices today will have been replaced by AI by the year 2050?

> I think **facial-recognition** technology **will have replaced** house and car keys long before 2050!

1.3 I GET WHAT YOU'RE SAYING ...

1 LISTENING

A Read the text message exchange. What is the relationship between the two texters? Why do you think that?

B 🔊 **1.06** **LISTEN FOR ATTITUDE** Listen to a conversation between two friends, Jeff and Dani. What does Jeff think of Dani's new app?

C 🔊 **1.06** **LISTEN FOR MAIN POINTS** Listen again and take notes on the positive and negative points they make about chatbots. Compare answers with a partner.

Positive: _____

_____

Negative: _____

_____

D **PAIR WORK** **THINK CRITICALLY** Look back at exercise 1A. Are you surprised that this is actually a chatbot conversation? Do you think computers will ever be able to understand and develop emotions? Why or why not?

2 PRONUNCIATION: Listening for contrastive stress

A 🔊 **1.07** **PAIR WORK** Listen. Pay attention to the underlined words. Why are they stressed?

Jeff   But it looks like a conversation with a <u>friend</u>.

Dani   Well, yeah, that's the point. It's a <u>virtual</u> friend.

Jeff   You mean a virtual <u>assistant</u>?

B 🔊 **1.08** <u>Underline</u> the words that have contrastive stress. Listen and check. Practice saying the sentences with your partner. Focus on word stress.

1   You have your own, personal talking machine – a learning machine!

2   I mean, why did they design it? Who did they design it for?

3   You can't always be there for me, but my bot can.

4   You're starting to talk about this bot as if it were a real person.

C (Circle) the correct words to complete the sentence.
When we want to clarify or correct what has been said, we often emphasize the word with the ¹*new / old* information and use a ²*lower / higher* pitch.

New Message   4:10 pm

> Yeah, but doesn't cooking take a crazy amount of time and effort?

> Not really. Going to the store takes longer!

> I can't stop thinking about ice cream. Chocolate maybe. 🍦

> I'd go for strawberry.

> What? I thought vanilla with chocolate sprinkles was your favorite.

> Most days. 😀

> Sugar cravings are the worst.

> I have salt cravings.

> Great. Now I want potato chips!

Send

3 SPEAKING SKILLS

A 🔊 **1.06** Listen to Jeff and Dani's conversation again. Check (✓) the expressions in the chart that they use.

> **Acknowledging arguments and proposing counterarguments**
>
> ☐ 1 **I can see how** that might be interesting, but …
> ☐ 2 **I understand what you're saying**, but I still don't get it.
> ☐ 3 **It's a valid point**, … but consider the other side.
> ☐ 4 **You have a good point** there.
> ☐ 5 **I get where you're coming from**, but …
> ☐ 6 **I hadn't really thought of it like that**. I guess you're right.
> ☐ 7 **I guess so**, but I'm still not convinced.
> ☐ 8 **You could look at it that way**, but that doesn't mean …

B Look at the expressions in the chart. Why does the speaker say the **bold** words? What purpose do they serve? What word is used to introduce a counterargument?

C GROUP WORK One student reads the statement. The person to their left acknowledges it and offers a counterargument. The next person to the left responds, etc. Change roles and start again. Use different phrases.

Statement: I don't think machines will ever be more intelligent than human beings.

> I hear what you're saying, but I think they can be better than us in some specific tasks.

> I get where you're coming from, but …

4 PRONUNCIATION: Saying expressions to show a counterargument

A 🔊 **1.09** Listen to the expressions and pay attention to the intonation. Then ⊙circle⊙ the correct words to complete the sentence below.

I understand what you're saying, but I still don't get it.   I know, I know, and it's a valid point.

Use a ¹*fall-rise / falling* intonation to show you question the other speaker's argument and a ²*fall-rise / falling* intonation to say what you think is true.

B 🔊 **1.10** Listen to the expressions. Check (✓) the ones where intonation suggests that the speaker is going to introduce a counterargument.

☐ 1 I guess so   ☐ 4 That may be true
☐ 2 I get where you're coming from   ☐ 5 I can see how that might work
☐ 3 You could look at it that way

C GROUP WORK Does technology always make life easier? Why or why not? Use the phrases in exercise 4B to introduce counterarguments with appropriate intonation in your discussion.

5 SPEAKING

A PAIR WORK THINK CRITICALLY Choose one of the statements and argue both sides of it. Acknowledge your partner's arguments and propose counterarguments.

- A good friend is always there for you.
- We spend far too much time in front of screens.
- Travel broadens the mind.

B Report back on your discussion. Summarize the arguments you were able to put forward in the time you had.

 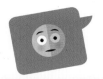

ROBOTICS TO THE RESCUE

1 READING

A   **PREDICT CONTENT FROM PICTURES**   Look at the pictures. Discuss how robots or robotics are being used in each situation to help humans. Read the article. Match the pictures to the correct sections.

ROBOTS AND HUMANS WORKING TOGETHER

When we think of robots, we often think of movies where humans have lost control and robots have taken over. But in reality, it isn't "us against them." Robots are helpmates in the workplace – more R2D2 than replicant!

Long-distance operations ___

For centuries, the mining industry has been dangerous work. More lives are lost and more workers are injured than in any other private industry. That's why engineers are working with robots to make mining safer. They're bringing the miners up to the surface and sending machines underground. The hope is that the death toll will have been reduced to zero in 20 years.

A great example of this effort is in the searing heat and dust of the red desert of western Australia. Here, robotics, AI, and satellite technology combine to allow engineers to control mining operations from the comfort of an office in Perth – 750 miles away. Driverless trucks, automated drilling machines, and complex logistical programs can all be run from a distance with minimal human intervention on the ground and no risk of injury or death.

They've got our backs ___

In the United States, tens of thousands of manufacturing workers are injured every year. They often perform the same physical tasks over and over, which causes strain to back, neck, and knee muscles and can lead to permanent disabilities. Millions of days of work are lost every year because of injuries. But robots – or more precisely, robotics – are helping reduce these figures.

Exosuits, or robotic vests, are being adopted for jobs that include heavy, repetitive work. In car manufacturing plants, for example, exosuits gently support the necks, backs, and shoulders of workers as they reach up into the engines of cars on the production line overhead. Watching the suit in action is truly amazing. It moves with the wearer and takes all the weight and strain of the manual work. Exosuits allow people to work more comfortably, which means they take fewer breaks and make fewer mistakes. One company estimates that the suits have increased productivity by 85%.

A helping hand ___

The service industry is introducing robots to provide, ironically, more personalized service. In some hotels in Japan, a robot helps out at reception. It greets guests and can translate requests in a number of different languages. It guides guests to their room and delivers messages, leaving human clerks free to deal with more complex transactions.

In the next 10 to 20 years, automation in dangerous jobs will have become the norm. Exosuits will have become common on the factory floor, no one will be left waiting at a hotel reception desk, and manufacturing workers will never again complain of a bad back!

B   **READ FOR DETAIL**   Read the article again. What are the three main ways that robots are used? What kind of technology does each one require?

C   **READ FOR ATTITUDE**   The editor of this article wants a new title that introduces the main topic, draws in readers, and also indicates the writer's attitude (skeptical, optimistic, neutral). Share your ideas with the class. Choose the best title.

D   GROUP WORK   **THINK CRITICALLY**   Can you think what the disadvantages might be for each use? How do you think the article might present the topic differently if it were written by a member of a labor union?

> **INSIDER** ENGLISH
>
> *I've got your back.* = I'm ready and willing to help or defend you.

2 WRITING

A **Read the essay. Which statement is it responding to? How do you know?**

Robots are stealing our jobs.   Robots will make workplaces safer.   Robots will eventually do creative work.

> ● ● ● ‹ ›   ⌕ 🏠
>
> Automation is inevitably going to be a feature of most workplaces. Machines are increasingly taking over dangerous jobs in industries **such as** mining and logging. They're already making jobs easier in industries that require a lot of manual labor, **namely** manufacturing and farming. They are also starting to appear in the service industry, helping employees deal with customers in, **for instance**, hotels and airports.
>
> Right now, automation feels good, helpful. But machines are moving from assisting humans to replacing them. **Take**, **for example**, jobs that consist of repetitive, heavy tasks – loading trucks, stocking shelves in stores, waiting tables in restaurants, **just to name a few**. What will human workers do when machines take over all those jobs?
>
> Optimists say that new jobs will replace these old jobs, that machines will never be as creative and innovative as people, and that the human touch cannot be replaced. I'm not convinced. I see the growth of automation as a direct threat to employment. We should prepare ourselves to face a world without work.

B **EXEMPLIFY ARGUMENTS** **Look at how the bold expressions in the essay are used to refer to examples. Then write sentences using the prompts below. Use a different expression each time.**

1   robots / dangerous tasks / working underground

   Robots will be able to take over dangerous tasks such as working underground.

2   exosuits / different settings / car manufacturing and hardware stores

3   robots / tasks / offering simultaneous translation and greeting guests

4   job loss / in key industries / construction and transportation

REGISTER CHECK

In informal writing and speaking, *like* can also introduce examples.

*I use my virtual assistant for stuff **like** reminders, shopping lists, looking something up online, playing music.*

WRITE IT

C **PLAN** **Read the statement below. Do you agree or disagree with it? What examples can you think of to support your opinion? What counterarguments can you imagine? Take notes.**

Artificial intelligence is going to take over our homes.

D **PAIR WORK** **Look again at the essay in exercise 2A and match each paragraph with its function.**

Paragraph 1: ___   **a**   Present argument(s)

Paragraph 2: ___   **b**   State a personal opinion

Paragraph 3: ___   **c**   Describe the current situation

Organize the ideas from your notes in the same way. Then work together to write a three-paragraph essay in about 200 words.

E **GROUP WORK** **In small groups, read each other's essays. What are some of the most interesting examples people used? Which examples do you think are the most effective in supporting their argument? Why?**

TIME TO SPEAK
Professor Robot?

A **DISCUSS** With one or two partners, look at the pictures. What is happening in each one? How might a robot helper improve the situation? Could a robot replace the human in any of them?

B **PREPARE** Choose one of the scenarios in the pictures (or a similar situation that you know about). Work together to create a proposal for a robot helper. Follow the steps below.

Step 1 Identify the main problem(s). Outline the tasks your robot will perform to address them and the technology required.

Step 2 Consider the social and psychological effects of a robot helper. What external appearance should the robot have to blend in with the environment?

Step 3 Prepare your proposal. Decide which features to emphasize, the order in which to present them, and who talks about what.

C **PRESENT** Share your proposal with the class. As you listen to the others, take notes and write at least one question to ask about each proposal.

D **AGREE** Discuss the proposals you have heard with students from other groups. Answer the questions.

■ Which robot design do you think is the most practical?

■ Which one(s) might be possible to make today?

■ Which idea would you be most likely to invest your own money in? Why?

E Share your ideas as a class. Do you all agree? If you had to choose one of the robot helpers to invest in as a class, which one would it be?

To check your progress, go to page 153.

USEFUL PHRASES

DISCUSS

A robot could certainly … as well as a person, but maybe not …

Once … , people won't … anymore.

PREPARE

It's going to need to be able to …

In order to … , it'll need …

PRESENT

We believe people will gradually …

With better AI, our robot could feasibly …

- discuss assumptions about behavior
- talk about assumptions related to age
- compare and discuss similar experiences
- write a report based on graphs
- conduct a survey about consumerism and labels

THE LABELS WE LIVE BY

2

START SPEAKING

A   Describe the people in the pictures in your own words. What can you tell about them from their appearance? Which of the labels in the box would you apply to each of them? Why? Look up any terms you don't know.

baby boomer	blue collar	conventional	hippie	middle class
millennial	nerd	realist	rebel	upper class

B   Why do we label people? Are labels generally harmless or hurtful? What are labels usually based on? Can you think of a situation where labels might serve a positive purpose? For ideas, watch Ryoko's video.

EXPERT SPEAKER

What do you think of Ryoko's ideas?

11

IS THAT REALLY ME?

1 LANGUAGE IN CONTEXT

A **PAIR WORK** Look at the quiz results. Do you ever do quizzes like these? Do you share your results? Why or why not?

B What do people get out of online personality quizzes? Read the magazine article and check your answers.

Personality for sale

Personality quizzes are all over social media. By now, most people will have taken quite a few of them and probably shared some of their results. Some people will share quiz results every single day! But will we really learn more about ourselves from *What historical figure are you?* than from *What animal would you be?* Probably not. In fact, personality quizzes won't ever provide any real insights because their real purpose is data mining.

It's easy to imagine the original idea: As a user eagerly takes quiz after quiz and shares the hilarious results across social media, quiz software will be quietly building a detailed profile of their style, tastes, likes, and dislikes. Algorithms will suggest other quizzes in order to fill in gaps. Software companies will then sell the profile to marketing companies.

Personality quizzes are the perfect vehicle because they play on our natural desire to be liked. They will nearly always return positive results. You'll be called **sincere** instead of humorless, fun and **chatty** instead of childish. Labels like **narrow-minded**, **aloof**, and **self-centered** don't exist in quiz world. Choose red as your favorite color, and you'll be labeled "the life of the party." You'll also soon see ads for red clothing, red sports equipment, and red cars!

Maybe a better test of personality is whether any of this matters to you. Now that you've read this article, will you continue to enjoy online quizzes (***open-minded***, *playful*), or will you never take another one (*cautious*, *strong-willed*, *independent*)?

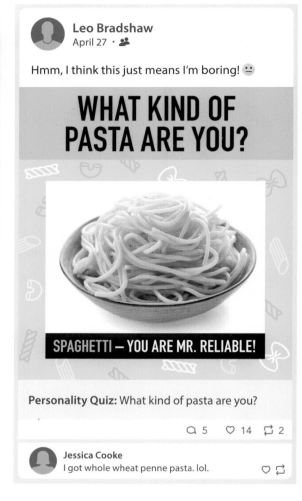

Leo Bradshaw
April 27 · 👥

Hmm, I think this just means I'm boring! 😐

WHAT KIND OF PASTA ARE YOU?

SPAGHETTI — YOU ARE MR. RELIABLE!

Personality Quiz: What kind of pasta are you?

💬 5   ♡ 14   ⇄ 2

Jessica Cooke
I got whole wheat penne pasta. lol.   ♡ ⇄

2 VOCABULARY: Describing personality

A 🔊 **1.11** Look at the **bold** adjectives in the article and match them to their synonyms below. Listen and check. Which two adjective pairs are opposites?

1 talkative _____
2 genuine _____
3 antisocial _____

4 rigid _____
5 insensitive _____
6 accepting _____

B ▶ Now go to page 142. Do the vocabulary exercises for 2.1.

C **PAIR WORK** **THINK CRITICALLY** Think of a fictional villain (from a book, TV show, movie, etc.). What are they like? Imagine the villain took a personality quiz on social media. How might the results put a positive spin on their negative qualities?

3 GRAMMAR: Uses of *will*

A Read the sentences in the grammar box. Match them with the uses below.

> ### Uses of *will*
>
> **A** Some people **will share** quiz results every single day!
>
> **B** But **will** we really **learn** more about ourselves from a quiz?
>
> **C** They **will** nearly always **return** positive results.
>
> **D** Now that you've read this article, **will** you **continue** to enjoy online quizzes?

Use *will* …

1 to make predictions, assumptions, or deductions about the future. Sentence *B*

2 to describe typical behavior or things that are true in general. Sentence ____

3 to express decisions about the future made at the point of speaking. Sentence ____

4 to criticize annoying habits or characteristics. Sentence ____

B ▶ Now go to page 130. Look at the grammar chart and do the grammar exercise for 2.1.

C PAIR WORK Read the statements. Respond to them using *will* or *won't*. Check your accuracy. Compare your sentences with a partner.

1 Personality quizzes on social media aren't meant to provide serious psychological analysis, and most people know that.

   Most people won't expect a serious psychological analysis from a social media personality quiz.

2 Advertisers want to target their ads to likely customers. Social media behavior is a good source of information about people's interests.

3 Social media users know more about data mining now and are more careful with their personal information. Software developers are continually working to find new ways to mine user data.

4 People like to be judged positively. They are more likely to click things that seem flattering or positive. App developers know this and consider it in their designs.

> ✓ **ACCURACY** CHECK
>
> **Use the past participle, not *to* + verb, when talking about something you assume has already happened.**
>
> *He hates to be late, so I'm sure he'll have to leave the office by now.* ✗
>
> *He hates to be late, so I'm sure he'll have left the office by now.* ✓

4 SPEAKING

A PAIR WORK THINK CRITICALLY Look at the six types of social media users. What do you think the labels mean? What can you assume, deduce, or predict about the people they're applied to?

| Collectors | Creators | Critics | Inactives | Joiners | Spectators |

Critics **will rate** every restaurant or store they go to, and they'll **be** sincere in their evaluations.

Spectators **won't comment** themselves, but they'll **be looking** at everything you post!

2.2 ACT YOUR AGE

1 LANGUAGE IN CONTEXT

A 🔊 **1.12** Look at the picture. Who do you think the people are, and how are they connected? Listen to the first part of a news interview with one of the men and check your answers.

🔊 **1.12 Audio script**

Host So, Manuel, would you mind telling us that story you told me earlier?

Manuel Sure. One day, I was talking with a mature student after class when a new supervisor came in and asked if I would leave the room so she could speak to my teacher.

Host What did you say?

Manuel Well, I just told her that, actually, I was the teacher here. She was really shocked. I mean, the student was older than me, so it's natural that she would think he was the teacher, but I could tell that she was **looking down on** me, you know?

Host Does that happen a lot?

Manuel It used to. I started teaching when I was 22. So in the early days, I would **run up against** attitudes like that a lot. There's this impression that millennials are irresponsible, so my colleagues thought a millennial wouldn't make a good teacher, that I just wouldn't **fit in with** the team. That's just ageism. I wouldn't accept it. I had to **stand up for** myself. I'd just tell them, hey, I was *recruited* for this job because I'm really good. Qualifications don't just **come down to** age.

Host But surely your coworkers know that.

Manuel You'd think so. Fortunately, that's all in the past. Now, things are fine.

2 VOCABULARY: Using three-word phrasal verbs

A 🔊 **1.12** Listen to the first part of the interview again and read along. Write the **bold** phrasal verbs next to their definitions below.

1 feel that you belong _____
2 defend _____
3 experience difficulties _____
4 think you are better than someone _____
5 be the most important part of _____

B 🔊 **1.13** Read the definitions below. Then listen to the second part of the interview and complete the three-word phrasal verbs that match the definitions.

1 deal with   face _____up to_____
2 tolerate   put _____
3 make fun of   mess _____
4 communicate successfully   get _____
5 use something easy or familiar   fall _____

C 🔊 **1.14** Listen and check your answers to exercises 2A and 2B.

D ▶ Now go to page 142. Do the vocabulary exercises for 2.2.

E PAIR WORK | THINK CRITICALLY Think about the interview. What advice does Manuel give to other people who have to fight against a negative label? What example does he give? What qualities do different people associate with millennials? Is that fair? Why or why not?

3 | GRAMMAR: Uses of *would*

A Read the sentences in the grammar box. Match them with the rules below.

> ### Uses of *would*
>
> **A** **Would** you mind telling us that story you told me earlier?
> **B** I **wouldn't** accept it. I had to stand up for myself.
> **C** You**'d** think so.
> **D** She asked if I **would** leave the room.
> **E** In the early days, I **would** run up against attitudes like that a lot.

Use *would* …

1 to refer to past habits or typical, expected behavior.   Sentence ___
2 to make a polite request.   Sentence ___
3 to express an opinion in a polite way.   Sentence ___
4 to report a statement or a question with *will*.   Sentence ___
5 to talk about what someone is willing or unwilling to do.   Sentence ___

B PAIR WORK What other ways can you express the ideas in the sentences with *would* from the interview? Restate them without using *would*.

> What's another way to say, "Would you mind telling us that story again?"

> "Please tell us that story again." Does that work?

C ▶ Now go to page 130. Look at the grammar chart and do the grammar exercise for 2.2.

D PAIR WORK Rewrite the prompts to create questions using *would*. Ask a partner your questions. Answer the questions your partner asks you.

1 what / do / weekends / childhood ?
2 feel comfortable / tell / something / personal ?
3 what / expectation / strangers / have / you ?
4 what / do / if / stranger / insult / you ?

4 | SPEAKING

A GROUP WORK THINK CRITICALLY Look at the actions in the box. At what age do you think a person is too old or too young to do them? For ideas, watch Ryoko's video.

> take/post a selfie   own a pet   drive
> go to music festivals   get a tattoo   vote
> start a business   wear jewelry
> ride a skateboard to and from work

EXPERT SPEAKER

What do you think Ryoko would say about the other actions?

B Think about your scenarios from exercise 4A. What attitudes might a young or old person run up against? How would you advise them to respond?

> I would tell them to stand up for themselves!

2.3 SAME HERE!

1 LISTENING

A | PAIR WORK | Look at the picture. What do you think is happening? Who isn't participating? Why not?

B 🔊 1.15 Listen to a conversation between Adam and Bella. Check (✓) the things they feel the same about.

- ☐ **a** Kids aren't affected much by labels.
- ☐ **b** Learning a language can change the way you see yourself.
- ☐ **c** People treat you differently when you can speak their language.

C 🔊 1.15 LISTEN FOR AGREEMENT Look at the expressions from the conversation. Write *E* for those that refer to <u>exactly the same</u> experiences and *D* for <u>different</u> experiences that produce the same feelings. Then listen again to check your answers.

1 I can relate to that. D
2 I know exactly what you mean! ___
3 That reminds me of the time when … ___
4 That's just like the time … ___
5 I know how you feel. ___
6 What a coincidence! ___

D | PAIR WORK | THINK CRITICALLY | Does learning a foreign language change the way others see you? How might it have an impact on the way you see yourself? What experiences have you had to support your opinion?

2 PRONUNCIATION: Listening for the intonation on interactional phrases

A 🔊 1.16 Listen. Does the intonation of the <u>underlined</u> phrases rise or fall?

1 <u>You know</u>, it's weird how you gain more confidence when you start speaking another language.
2 If they label you an introvert, that's how you behave, <u>right</u>?

B 🔊 1.17 Listen. <u>Underline</u> the phrases you hear that have rising intonation.

1 I was always the quiet kid at school, you know, the one who never had much to say.
2 It's amazing! I'm a more confident person, you know?
3 The best thing is that people respect you more when you can speak their language, don't you think?

C (Circle) the correct word to complete the sentence.

Interactional phrases, which have little real meaning but keep the listener interested and involved, usually have a *rising* / *falling* intonation.

3 SPEAKING SKILLS

A 🔊 1.18 Complete the expressions that Adam and Bella used in their conversation. Listen and check.

Discussing similar experiences	
1 I hear _____ .	6 That's _____ like the time (when) …
2 I can _____ to that.	7 I know how you _____ .
3 I know exactly _____ you mean.	8 _____ here, …
4 Has that been the _____ for you?	9 _____ me about it!
5 That _____ me of the time (when) …	10 What a _____ !

B   GROUP WORK   **One student reads the statement below. The others say whether they share the experience and add their own statements to keep the conversation going.**

Statement: At school, I was the "teacher's pet." All the other kids hated me.

> Tell me about it! My aunt was our teacher, so I was definitely the teacher's pet. It can be hard to shake off a label like that.

> I know what you mean. I was always the troublemaker. Even when I was good, teachers saw me as "the bad kid."

4   PRONUNCIATION: Saying stressed syllables beginning with /p/, /k/, /t/

A   🔊 1.19   **Listen to the /p/, /k/, and /t/ sounds in the sentences. Are the <u>underlined</u> ones different from the ⊙circled⊙ ones?**

1   My o<u>p</u>inion is tha(t) mos(t) people in this <u>c</u>oun(t)ry spea(k) a bi(t) of English.

2   <u>K</u>ids can find i(t) hard (t)o sha(k)e off a label li(k)e tha(t).

3   <u>T</u>ell me abou(t) i(t)! My aun(t) was my <u>t</u>eacher…

B   🔊 1.20   PAIR WORK   <u>Underline</u> the /p/, /k/, and /t/ sounds in stressed syllables. Listen and check. **Practice the conversation with a partner.**

A   What do you think? Could you teach English to kids?

B   Tough question! I like children, and I'm quite patient, but the parents can be too demanding at times.

A   Tell me about it! You've got to have a really strong character to put up with some of them.

C   PAIR WORK   **With your partner, add two lines to the conversation above using as many /p/, /k/, and /t/ sounds in stressed syllables as you can. Join another pair of students and read your conversations.**

5   SPEAKING

A   PAIR WORK   **Read the statements about language learning and explain whether you can relate.**

I have a hard time with humor when I speak another language. I'm funnier in my own language.

I learn a lot by watching TV shows and reading the subtitles.

B   GROUP WORK   THINK CRITICALLY   **Join another pair of students and share your ideas. Create your own statements about language learning based on your discussion.**

C   **Share your statements with the class. Is there an experience that you all have in common?**

1 READING

A **PREDICT CONTENT** Look at the product labels in the article. What do they have in common? Read the headline of the article. What do you think the article will be about? Read it to check your answer.

IT'S NOT NATURAL

You're in your local grocery store to buy a can of soup. You're looking for a healthy option, so you dutifully read the product labels. But now the choice gets even more confusing. One says that the ingredients are "locally sourced," another says "organic," and another claims it is "100% natural." All that sounds great, but are "free-range" eggs really better for you? Is "grass-fed beef" also "hormone-free"? What is an "artificial color" anyway? In other words, which labels actually represent real nutritional value, and which are just the latest food fad?

In general, the vaguer the term, the more difficult it is to prove. For example, the United States Department of Agriculture (USDA) was recently forced to develop a definition and guidelines regarding the label "organic." To use "organic" on the packaging, a product must have 70% organic ingredients. And to be "100% organic," products should have no added chemicals, synthetics, pesticides, or genetically engineered substances.

The label "natural," however, is a lot trickier, as there is no legal definition, meaning that even obviously unhealthy foods can be marketed as "natural" and nobody can say it isn't true. This has led to many lawsuits, which focus not only on food, but on other products that also carry the "natural" label.

What makes the "natural" label particularly complicated is that it is associated in our minds with the idea of "healthy." It brings to mind simple, unprocessed foods cooked at home and put on the family dinner table

by mom. Consumers will pay a lot for that fantasy, so companies want "natural" on their product labels – and they would rather *not* have it legally defined.

The "natural" debate has been with us for a long time, but the latest food fad seems to be "free-from" products. The strange thing is that you now see these labels on products that would never contain the target substance in the first place. You can even buy "sugar-free" water!

Customers are choosing "free-from" products because they assume the product is healthier for them, but actually, the opposite might be true. For example, research shows that following a gluten-free diet when you have no medical need for it can lead to weight gain. Why? Because gluten-free substitutes are often higher in fat and lower in protein. Also, if a food is perceived as healthy, people are likely to eat more of it!

The irony is that in the past we measured the healthfulness of food by the nutrients it contained. Now we measure by what a product claims *not* to have. If all the labels on the supermarket shelves make you dizzy, the best advice is not to go for "fat-free," but "fad-free." You can never go wrong with fresh fruits and vegetables from your local farmers market.

INSIDER ENGLISH

makes me dizzy = is too much to think about clearly

B **PAIR WORK** **READ FOR MAIN IDEAS** Answer the questions.
1 What is the difference between the labels "organic" and "natural"?
2 What assumption do people make about "free-from" products?
3 What is the writer's general advice about choosing products?

C **PAIR WORK** **IDENTIFYING PURPOSE** What do you think is the writer's main intention in this article? Who do you think is the target audience? Why?

D **GROUP WORK** **THINK CRITICALLY** How often do you read product labels on food packaging or health and beauty products? Do you think the labels are misleading and dangerous or helpful and informative? Why? What advice would you give consumers about understanding labels?

2 WRITING

A **Look at the graphs. Match each graph to the information it displays. Read the report and check your answers.**

1 most popular "free-from" products

2 popularity of "free-from" products in the U.K.

3 reasons why people buy "free-from" products

4 reasons why people don't buy "free-from" products

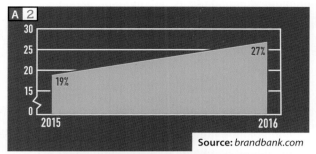
Source: *brandbank.com*

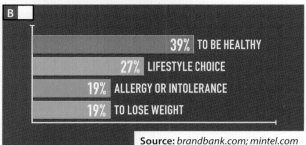
Source: *brandbank.com; mintel.com*

Source: *mintel.com*

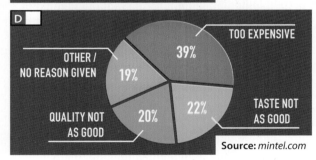
Source: *mintel.com*

THE "FREE-FROM" PHENOMENON

In the U.K., "free-from" products now represent the fastest-growing food and drink category and are currently worth £122.9 million.

As can be seen from graph A, 27% of U.K. residents regularly shop in the "free-from" aisle. This figure increased by 8% in one year. This would indicate that there is a strong consumer trend towards buying foods that are perceived as healthy.

Graph B presents the reasons for this trend. It indicates that most "free-from" consumers (39%) choose these products in order to feel healthier, while only 19% cite an actual allergy or intolerance. This would seem to be a valuable insight for food product marketers.

....

The data in these graphs leads us to conclude that "free-from" products are here to stay on our supermarket shelves, and their popularity will continue to rise.

B **EXPLAIN DATA** **Look at the expressions for referring to data. Read the report again and complete them.**

1 As can be *inferred* / *observed* / _____ from X, …

2 X *shows* / *points out* / *highlights* / *depicts* / _____ the reasons for / causes of …

3 X *implies* / *reveals* / *suggests* / _____ that …

4 The data *would suggest* / *confirms* / *indicates* / _____ that …

 **WRITE IT**

C **PLAN** **You're going to complete the report in exercise 2A by writing the two missing paragraphs. With a partner, analyze the paragraphs on graphs A and B.**

■ What information comes first?   ■ How does each paragraph end?

Discuss how this style can be used to present the information in graph C and graph D.

D **Write the two missing paragraphs on your own.**

E **PAIR WORK** **THINK CRITICALLY** **Exchange papers with your partner. Did you both reference all the data from the graphs? Did you draw similar conclusions?**

TIME TO SPEAK
Labeled out

A **RESEARCH** With a partner, look at the pictures and think about some popular designer labels for each product. What information do shoppers usually assume based on the label (quality, stylishness, fit, etc.)? Are labels an important factor in your own shopping decisions? What else influences you?

B Look at the responses on a shopping blog. What questions do you think were asked? Which answer do you most relate to? Why?

 I shop for brand-name clothes online or at outlet stores. It's much cheaper than buying the same thing at the mall.
💬 2   ♡ 12

 I wouldn't buy something just because of the label. I only care about how it looks on me.
💬 1   ♡ 11   ⇄ 3

 If you buy a recognized label, you know that the product is well made and in style. It's worth paying extra for that.
💬 9   ♡ 48

 The people in my office all dress very nicely. If I wore an off-brand suit, they wouldn't say anything, but they would be thinking that I don't look professional enough.
💬 5   ♡ 20   ⇄ 9

C **PREPARE** Work with another pair to write ten survey questions on brands and labels. Decide on five to use for your survey. Use your work from exercise B for ideas and consider the topics below.

labels and social status   personal attitudes on famous labels

social pressures around fashion   the importance of advertising

D **DISCUSS** Conduct your survey individually. Each person in your group should survey at least three people, for a total of at least 12 responses per question. Then collate your data and highlight the most interesting results. Responses won't be uniform, so draw conclusions and note patterns.

E **PRESENT** Form new groups of four. Take turns presenting the results from your surveys. Discuss the most interesting results from the four different surveys and create a statement that summarizes each of them.

F Share your statements with the class. Discuss them and agree on a few conclusions that can be drawn from the surveys.

▶▶ *To check your progress, go to page 153.* ▶▶

USEFUL PHRASES

DISCUSS

Of the people I surveyed, 75% said …

Only one in four respondents agreed that …

The majority of our responses seem to point to …

PRESENT

In general, the survey data indicates …

However, it would appear that …

It would be fair to conclude that labels …

UNIT OBJECTIVES

- discuss past actions and their present results
- react to past situations
- describe a negative experience; offer sympathy and reassurance
- write a short story based on a set of facts
- discuss and present an alternate history

START SPEAKING

A People often say "Hindsight is 20/20." What does this mean? Use a dictionary or your phone to help you. Do you agree with the expression? Why or why not?

B Now look at the picture. What is happening? Why do you think the man chose to do this? In hindsight, do you think he would make the same choice again? Why or why not?

EXPERT SPEAKER

Would you say hindsight has helped Andrea learn from this experience?

C Think of a time when you did something that didn't end well. What were the consequences? Do you regret it? For ideas, watch Andrea's video.

I TOLD YOU SO!

1 LANGUAGE IN CONTEXT

A **PAIR WORK** Look at the meme. Do you think it's funny? In what kinds of situations are you likely to hear "I told you so"? When was the last time someone said it to you?

B 🔊 **1.21** Listen to part of a podcast about "hindsight bias." What is it? What are the dangers of it?

> I guess the bleach was a bad idea.
>
> I told you so.

GLOSSARY
bleach (*n*) a chemical whitener used for laundry

🔊 **1.21 Audio script**

> "I told you so."
>
> "Well, if you'd mentioned all this road work, I would've gone a different way."
>
> "Well, if you'd been listening, you'd have heard me say that the highway is always better, and we wouldn't be sitting in this traffic jam right now!"

"I told you so" – one of the most annoying phrases in the English language, especially when it isn't true! Did she really **foresee** what was going to happen? No, she just got lucky. This is a classic example of "hindsight bias."

Humans have the ability to **review** and **reconsider** past experiences and **analyze** the decisions we made. This is how we learn from our mistakes. Hindsight bias interferes with this process, making it difficult to accurately **evaluate** past situations. If you're convinced you knew how something would eventually turn out, then you **dismiss** any doubts you might have had beforehand, you **reject** alternative scenarios that might have led to the same outcome, and you **fixate** on a single explanation.

Hindsight bias also makes it easy to **presume** you know what's going to happen in the future. If you're convinced there was only one way to **interpret** a past situation, you're less likely to **envision** creative solutions for new problems. You just go with the first idea that comes to you and **disregard** the advice of others. And soon, *you're* the one hearing "I told you so."

2 VOCABULARY: Thought processes

A 🔊 **1.22** Look at the **bold** verbs in the script. How are they used in context? Match them to the categories. Listen and check.

1 thinking about the future: _____ , _____

2 examining something: _____ , _____ , _____

3 re-examining something: _____ , _____

4 not accepting something: _____ , _____ , _____

5 an unproductive way to think: _____ , _____

B ▶ Now go to page 143. Do the vocabulary exercises for 3.1.

C **PAIR WORK** **THINK CRITICALLY** Which thought processes would you use to write a summary of a long text? To choose a vacation destination? To examine a friend's unusually bad behavior?

> First, you need to **analyze** the text for main ideas and then **evaluate** which points support them.

3 GRAMMAR: Variations on past unreal conditionals

A **Read the sentences in the grammar box. Complete the rules.**

> **Variations on past unreal conditionals**
>
> Well, if you**'d mentioned** all this road work, I **would've gone** a different way.
>
> Well, if you**'d been listening**, you**'d have heard** me, …
>
> … and we **wouldn't be sitting** in this traffic jam right now.

1 To refer to an unreal action in the past, use *if* + _____ + past participle. To describe an unreal action in progress in the past, use *if* + _____ + *been* + verb + *-ing*.

2 To describe the imagined reaction in the past, use _____ + *have* + past participle.

3 To describe the imagined reaction in the present, use _____ + verb OR _____ + *be* + verb + *-ing*.

4 In these sentences, *'d* could be a contraction of *would* or _____ .

B **Now go to page 131. Look at the grammar chart and do the grammar exercise for 3.1.**

C 🔊 **1.23** | PAIR WORK | **Listen to the story of someone who suffered as a result of hindsight bias. How could he have acted differently to change the outcome? Write three sentences using *if* to talk about possible alternative scenarios.**

4 SPEAKING

A | GROUP WORK | **What do you think is happening in each situation? Choose one of them and imagine the back story (the events that led up to it). Write three or four sentences to tell the story. Then give your paper to another group.**

B **Read the story from the other group. Discuss how things could have turned out differently. Write five sentences with *if*. Share them with the class. How many different scenarios did your group come up with?**

> If the woman **hadn't left** her purse in her car, …

C THINK CRITICALLY **Why is it important to consider multiple possible back stories? What are some different ways that doing so can be helpful?**

1   LANGUAGE IN CONTEXT

A   **PAIR WORK**   Would you describe yourself as a relaxed or a nervous person? How would your closest friends describe you? Do the quiz. Do your answers support your self-description?

MELLOW **OR** MELODRAMATIC?

How good are you at handling awkward situations? When you've done something foolish, do you stay **composed** or do you get **flustered**? When someone offends you, are you **gracious** and **forgiving**, or are you **spiteful** and determined to get even? Take the quiz to find out your true temperament.

QUESTION 1: You arrive home and realize you left your house keys at work. What do you do?

A You get **hysterical** and start to cry. You should have checked that you had your keys before you left! This is a complete disaster!

B Ugh! You should have given an extra key to a neighbor. You call friends until one of them invites you to stay at their place.

C You're **resourceful**; you can solve this problem. Ah-ha! You call a coworker who is working late and lives nearby. She drops off your keys an hour later. You feel **victorious**!

QUESTION 2: Over lunch, you tell some friends an embarrassing story about your new boss. As you're leaving, you see her sitting at the table right behind you.

A You just want to crawl under a rock. You knew she could have been having lunch then, too! Why didn't you look around first?

B You smile and say hello. It was just a **harmless** little story. She might not have been offended by it. She may have even liked that you were talking about her.

C You walk away as if nothing happened. There's no reason to feel **defensive** or guilty. She may not have heard you.

B   Compare your answers as a class. Would you say that you generally go with the flow or blow things out of proportion? What are some other possible reactions to the situations in the quiz? For ideas, watch Andrea's video.

EXPERT SPEAKER

How are Andrea's answers different from the options in the quiz?

2   VOCABULARY: Describing emotional reactions

FIND IT

A   🔊 **1.24**   **PAIR WORK**   Look at the **bold** words in the quiz. Write them in the correct category in the chart below. Look up any words that you're not sure about. Then listen and check.

Positive reaction	Negative reaction	Context dependent
mellow	melodramatic	

B   ▶ Now go to page 143. Do the vocabulary exercises for 3.2.

C   **PAIR WORK**   Read the situations in the box. Choose one and prepare a short conversation to act out for another pair. Can they guess what emotional reactions you're expressing?

an accident that is your fault	an argument with your parent(s)
a surprise party for you	winning a prize

3 GRAMMAR: Commenting on the past

A Read the sentences in the grammar box. Complete the rules with words from the sentences.

> **Commenting on the past**
>
> You **should have checked** that you had your keys before you left.
> You **should have given** an extra key to a neighbor.
> You knew she **could have been having** lunch then, too.
> She **might not have been offended** by it.
> She **may not have heard** you.

1 You can use _____ , _____ , and _____ to discuss possible alternative scenarios in the past.

2 You can use _____ and _____ *not* to criticize a past action or lack of action.

3 To describe actions in progress, use *could/may/might/should* + _____ + _____ + verb + *-ing*.

4 You can also use the passive voice: *could/may/might/should* + _____ + _____ + past participle.

B ▶ **Now go to page 131. Look at the grammar chart and do the grammar exercise for 3.2.**

C Read question 3 from the quiz on page 24. Write three answer choices using *could have*, *may have*, *might have*, or *should have*. Check your accuracy. Share your answer choices with the class. Who came up with the best ones?

> ✓ **ACCURACY** CHECK
>
> Remember to use the past participle after *have* when talking about the past.
> You should have ~~tell~~ her. ✗
> You should have told her. ✓

> **QUESTION 3:** You are about to go into an important meeting where several people are waiting for you. Your office phone rings, and you answer it without thinking. It's your mother. She doesn't sound upset, but she says she wants to talk to you about something important.

4 SPEAKING

A PAIR WORK Think of another situation with different possible reactions and create QUESTION 4 for the quiz along with three answer choices.

> How about, you're walking your dog and it scares a little boy and makes him cry?

> That's a good one. The **mellow** answer could be "You're not **flustered** by it. The little boy **could have been crying** about something else."

B GROUP WORK Share your quiz question with two other pairs of students. Do they like your answer choices? What other reactions might they have had?

A COMPLETE DISASTER!

1 LISTENING

A **PAIR WORK** Look at the picture at the bottom of the page. What has just happened? How do you think the person feels? What problems do you think this might cause?

B 🔊 **1.25** **LISTEN FOR ATTITUDE** Listen to two conversations in which Ruben tells two different coworkers a story. Answer the questions.

1 What exactly happened with the coffee?
2 What else went wrong?

3 How does Ruben feel about the situation?
4 Do you think he might be exaggerating?

C 🔊 **1.25** **THINK CRITICALLY** Listen again. In what ways are the two versions of the story different? Why do you think that is? Who is more supportive, Claire or Amelia?

D **PAIR WORK** Have you ever found yourself in a similar situation? Were your friends supportive? What did they say?

2 PRONUNCIATION: Listening for weak forms in complex verb phrases

> **!** You can use *literally* to exaggerate a description. *I literally froze!*

A 🔊 **1.26** Listen and <u>underline</u> the complex verb phrases.

1 Don't you think you could be overreacting?
2 I must have brought the wrong one.
3 I'd emailed it to myself.

B 🔊 **1.27** **PAIR WORK** Unscramble the sentences. Circle any words in the complex verb phrases that should be stressed. Listen and check.

1 day / been / it / had / a / terrible _____
2 could / been / worse / have / things _____
3 me / had / wish / listened / I / you / to _____
4 have / hurt / could / someone / been _____
5 sense / made / that / more / would / have _____

C Circle the correct words to complete the sentences.

In a complex verb phrase, auxiliaries are usually ¹*stressed / unstressed*. Modals can be stressed or unstressed, but if they are not being used for deduction, they are usually ²*stressed / unstressed*.

3   SPEAKING SKILLS

A   **Read the expressions in the chart from the conversations in exercise 1B. Match each heading from the box to the correct column and write them in.**

Describing a bad experience   Offering sympathy and reassurance

It can't have been that bad.	It was a total/unmitigated disaster!
I'm sure it just felt that way.	I wish I'd just stayed in bed today.
I'll bet no one even noticed.	I just couldn't believe this was happening!
We've all been there.	It was the worst presentation ever!
Everybody (goes blank) now and then.	You haven't heard the worst part yet.
I think you're blowing it out of proportion.	Everything that could possibly go wrong did go wrong.
Things are never as bad as you think they are.	
You'll see – everything'll be just fine.	

B   **PAIR WORK**   **Imagine that Claire and Amelia just told you about Ruben's "disaster." You go and talk to him and reassure him. Act out the conversation two times, taking turns as Ruben.**

4   PRONUNCIATION: Using intonation to show emphasis

A   🔊 **1.28** **Listen to the sentences and notice intonation. Does it fall or rise at the end?**

1   I just couldn't believe this was happening!

2   It was the worst presentation ever!

B   🔊 **1.29**   **PAIR WORK**   **Listen. Which reading has more emphasis? Check (✓) A or B. Practice the ones you checked with a partner.**

1   It was such a mess!   ☐ A   ☐ B

2   Nice try!   ☐ A   ☐ B

3   I can't believe it!   ☐ A   ☐ B

4   I wish I'd never bought it!   ☐ A   ☐ B

5   We got there two hours late!   ☐ A   ☐ B

6   It was broken, I'm telling you, totally broken!   ☐ A   ☐ B

C   **PAIR WORK**   **Take turns giving details of what went wrong in the situations below. Be creative and use intonation to show emphasis.**

■   You forgot your best friend's birthday.

■   You borrowed your roommate's sweater and got ink on it.

■   You stayed in a terrible hotel.

5   SPEAKING

A   **PAIR WORK**   **Read the situations. Choose one to act out. Take turns explaining what happened (add as many details as you want) and reassuring your partner. Then act out the other one.**

■   You just damaged your father's car. (Think about how and where it happened and the extent of the damage.)

■   You just forwarded a personal email to the whole office by mistake. (Think about what was in the email.)

B   **GROUP WORK**   **THINK CRITICALLY**   **Tell the class about the situations and your partner's response. Whose situation was the most awful? Who gave the best advice? In a situation like this, what's more important, sympathy or honesty? Why do you think so?**

3.4 TOO GOOD TO BE TRUE

1 READING

A **PREDICT CONTENT** Read the headlines of the two "clickbait" news stories. What do you think happened in each one? Read the stories to check your ideas.

MAN SAVES BABY – AGAIN!

One day in the 1930s, in Detroit, Michigan, Joseph Figlock was walking down the street when a baby fell from a window in the building he was passing. He caught the baby and saved his life. One year later, on the exact same street, the exact same baby again fell out of the exact same window. And yes, you guessed it – our hero, Joseph Figlock, just happened to be there! Figlock again caught the baby and saved his life for a second time.

TWO GIRLS, ONE BALLOON, DOUBLE LIVES!

Ten-year-old Laura Buxton released a balloon with her name and address on it. More than 220 kilometers away, another 10-year-old girl found the balloon in her backyard. Her name was Laura Buxton, too! When the girls met, they realized they didn't just share a name. They looked exactly alike – tall and thin with long brown hair – and were even dressed the same in blue jeans and pink sweaters. They even had the same pets: a gray rabbit, a black Labrador, and a guinea pig!

B **EVALUATE CONTENT** Do you believe the stories are true? Why or why not? Read the report on the two stories from a fact-checking site. Did the stories happen exactly as they were reported?

FACT CHECKER

What's new **Top 50** **Videos** **Archive**

November 8

We've had a lot of requests today to investigate two clickbait stories that just seem too good to be true. In both cases, the reports may not have been 100% faithful to the facts, but there's enough truth in them to make them incredible coincidences!

Man saves baby – again!

The story claims that the same man saved the life of the same baby twice in the same place. Let's look at the facts:

🔍 Joseph Figlock was a street cleaner, so he was not on that street by chance. He worked there regularly.

🔍 The baby did fall from a window, but it was not caught by the street cleaner. It landed on Figlock and then fell to the ground. It was injured but not killed.

🔍 A little over a year later (not exactly one year), Figlock was cleaning another street when a different baby fell from a different window. Again, both were injured, but they survived.

So, in hindsight, not quite the incredible coincidence that was reported, but if Mr. Figlock hadn't been working on those two days on those two streets, those two babies probably would have died!

Two girls, one balloon, double lives

The second story is about one girl who released a balloon and found her "twin." But let's take a closer look:

🔍 "Laura" was a very common name for girls of that age. And "Buxton" is a fairly common family name where the girls lived.

🔍 The balloon was found by a farmer who knew the second Laura's family, and he gave it to the second Laura.

🔍 The second Laura was nine, almost ten, and it's not unusual for girls of the same age to have similar hairstyles and clothes.

🔍 Black Labradors were one of the most common family dogs in the area, and lots of children have pet rabbits and guinea pigs.

Of course, these stories carefully leave out the non-coincidental details. For example, the two Lauras didn't have the same favorite color or the same number of brothers and sisters. But it's true that if the farmer hadn't found the balloon in the field and recognized Laura's name, the two girls wouldn't be friends today.

C **THINK CRITICALLY** Do you think it's important to fact-check stories like these? Why or why not? In what other situations do you think it is or isn't important to fact-check details and sources? How can you do that?

2 WRITING

A   **Read the story about another strange coincidence. Compare it with the notes on the right. Which pieces of information from the notes did the writer leave out of the story? Why?**

New	World	Science	Technology	Entertainment

One Christmas, twin sisters Lorraine and Levinia, who lived about ten minutes apart by car, **each** suddenly decided, on the spur of the moment, to deliver the other her Christmas present. It was cold and snowy, and the country roads between their **two** houses were dangerously icy. **Neither** of the sisters had snow chains on their tires, and **both** ended up sliding on the ice and crashing head-on into another car. And guess who was in the other car? Yes, that's right. They crashed into each other! They were **both** taken to the hospital, where they were **both** found to have broken their left leg. And of course, they ended up spending Christmas **together** in the **same** hospital!

- Twin sisters, Christmas
- Heading to each other's house to deliver presents
- One in large SUV, other in small sports car
- One coming from work, the other from shopping
- One on her own, other with her kids
- Snow/ice; both no chains on tires
- Crash happened about 8 p.m.
- One broke left arm and leg, other just left leg
- One stayed overnight, other had surgery, stayed two weeks

B   **CREATE COHESION Look at the bold words and phrases in the story in exercise 2A. Notice how they are used to highlight the coincidences. Use them to complete the story below.**

¹ _____ nine-year-old twin brothers, Mitch and Toby, were playing ² _____ in their backyard. They were racing each other down the slide. Suddenly, they ³ _____ fell, Mitch from the top of the slide and Toby at the base. The ⁴ _____ of them were taken to the hospital. They were ⁵ _____ very brave, and ⁶ _____ of them cried. However, the doctors found that ⁷ _____ of them had broken their left arm in exactly the ⁸ _____ place. The brothers went home with their arms in casts, and ⁹ _____ of them was allowed to play on the slide again until they'd ¹⁰ _____ gotten better!

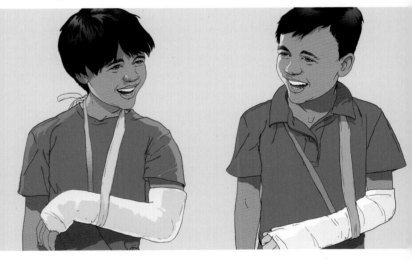

C   PAIR WORK **Student A: Go to page 157. Student B: Go to page 159. Read about a strange coincidence.**

D   PLAN **You're going to write a short story of about 100 words based on the set of facts you read in exercise 2C. Look again at the stories in exercises 2A and 2B.**

- How does each story begin?
- In what order are the events of the story presented?
- How are the coincidences emphasized?

Think about how to organize the facts of your story and emphasize the coincidences similarly. Then write your short story.

E   PAIR WORK THINK CRITICALLY **Read each other's stories. Which story is more believable? Why? What improvements can you suggest for your partner's story?**

3.5 TIME TO SPEAK
The ripple effect

LESSON OBJECTIVE
- discuss and present an alternate history

A   **DISCUSS**   With a partner, look at the picture of ripples on water. What do you think "the ripple effect" means when talking about our lives? Think of something that has caused ripples in your life recently. What was it and how did it affect you? What could you have done differently? How would that have changed things?

B   Think about the ripple effect on a larger scale. Read the "what if" scenarios. Choose one of them and discuss possible ripples that would have or might have resulted. Take notes as you go.

- What if the internet had never been invented? How would your childhood have been different?
- What if you had lived 100 years ago? How would your life have been different? What choices would you have had? What options wouldn't you have had?
- What if you had been born in a different country (choose one)? What would your childhood have been like there? Would you have made the same choices? *Could* you have made the same choices?

   No internet – would have played outside more, probably would have become interested in science, might have chosen to study biology instead of math, …

C   **DECIDE**   Join two other pairs to form a group of six. Present your ideas and decide which scenario is the most interesting in terms of the changes it might have caused in life today. Choose one scenario to tell the class about.

D   **PRESENT**   Share your scenario and at least three ripple effects with the class. Listen to the other groups. Ask questions to explore more possible ripple effects.

E   **AGREE**   Discuss the scenarios presented and decide which one would have the greatest ripple effect – on your own lives and on society as a whole.

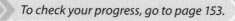

To check your progress, go to page 153.

USEFUL PHRASES

DISCUSS

If that were the case, I probably wouldn't have …

My whole world would have been different.

DECIDE

We explored the second scenario, and we figured …

We should present your scenario because …

PRESENT

It would have been a disaster because …

We might have stopped … before it happened.

REVIEW 1 (UNITS 1–3)

1 VOCABULARY

A **Complete the paragraph using the correct form of the words in parentheses ( ).**

Most recent developments in technology have [1] _unquestionably_ (question) come about thanks to artificial [2] _____ (intelligent). Advances in facial [3] _____ (recognize) mean computers can lip read more efficiently than humans. They are also getting [4] _____ (progress) better at reading human emotions. They can already detect anger, sadness, and joy. Voice-[5] _____ (active) is proving helpful in many ways, from being able to ask your phone for directions to ordering groceries through your virtual [6] _____ (assist). And our computers are getting more [7] _____ (talk), too! They don't only answer your questions; they also initiate conversations. It seems they're not the cold, [8] _____ (sensitive) machines of yesterday. Who knows – your computer could [9] _____ (potential) become your new best friend!

B **What new AI developments would you like to see? Complete the thoughts with at least one of the words in parentheses ( ) and your own ideas.**

1 In the future, robots … (undoubtedly / ultimately)

_____

2 Computer-generated speech has the potential to … (radically / drastically)

_____

3 Health care and medicine will/won't benefit … (progressively / increasingly)

_____

4 Image recognition could … (feasibly / markedly)

_____

5 (Open-minded / Narrow-minded) people might just …

_____

6 AI could even help (aloof / antisocial / rigid / self-centered) people …

_____

2 GRAMMAR

A Ⓒircle **the correct options to complete the article about life in the future.**

Want to know what the future holds? Ask a sci-fi fan! They [1]*will / do* always give you the most imaginative answers. Here are five of their craziest predictions:

> You'll [2]*be checking / have checked* your email on your contact lenses.

> Scientists will [3]*be finding / have found* a way to clone dinosaurs.

> Movies will [4]*be using / have used* only computer-generated images instead of actors – and these fake actors will [5]*be winning / have won* all the awards at the Oscars!

> Doctors will [6]*be using / have used* bathroom mirrors to diagnose medical conditions using high-definition cameras and special operating systems.

> We [7]*probably won't / won't probably* have robot butlers, but AI [8]*will eventually replace / will replace eventually* most of the gadgets we use now.

Which of these predictions do you think [9]*are definitely going to / are going to definitely* come true, and which are only for the movies?

B PAIR WORK **Look at the question at the end of the article in exercise 2A. How would you answer it? Think of three more crazy predictions for the future. Use the topics in the box to help you.**

| education | food | houses | pets | sports | transportation | vacations |

3 VOCABULARY

A   Complete the survey results with the correct form of the words in the box.

| defensive | dismiss | flustered | harmless | look | mess | presume | put |

What ruins your day?
We asked readers to share their thoughts. Here's what they said …

① People who act all superior and _____ down on you for no reason.

② When you make a suggestion and your boss just _____ it without even considering it.

③ When you try to make a _____ joke but someone gets offended by it. Then you feel _____ and try to explain, but that just makes it worse.

④ When you're in a quiet place and drop something and everybody turns to look at what made that noise, and they realize it was you, and you get _____ and drop something else, and all you want to do is crawl under a rock!

⑤ When people _____ you don't know what you're talking about just because you're young, but actually you know more than they do!

⑥ Roommates who _____ around with my stuff. They should keep their hands to themselves!

⑦ Noisy neighbors – they're the worst! Why should I have to _____ up with their loud music all night!

B   [PAIR WORK] **Do you identify with any of the complaints above? Think of more things that can ruin your day and explain them. Use vocabulary from Units 1 to 3 if you can.**

4 GRAMMAR

A   Complete the sentences with *had, could, might, should,* or *would*. Use contractions where possible.

I knew there was something wrong when my boss started staying late at the office. He [1]_____ normally be the first to leave, and sometimes he [2]_____ not even come in at all. One night, I stayed late, too. I told him I [3]_____ help him finish our paperwork. At eight o'clock, a man showed up and went into my boss's office and closed the door. I know I [4]_____n't have done it, but I pressed my ear to the door and listened to their conversation. They were arguing. I guess it [5]_____ have been about something totally innocent, but it didn't sound like it. Then I heard the man pick up a chair and let out an angry growl! I [6]_____ have knocked, but I rejected that idea and just ran into the room and pushed the man down. You [7]_____ have done the same if it [8]_____ been you! But I soon learned that I [9]_____n't interpreted things correctly. My boss and his friend were rehearsing for a play. If only I [10]_____ minded my own business!

B   **What would you have done in the same situation? How do you think the situation could have been avoided? Use modals to write three sentences about alternate scenarios in the past.**

32

- discuss the value of changing perspective
- talk about how eyes function in humans and animals
- discuss problems caused by staring at screens
- write a personal profile statement for a résumé
- create and present an action plan for a project

CLOSE UP

4

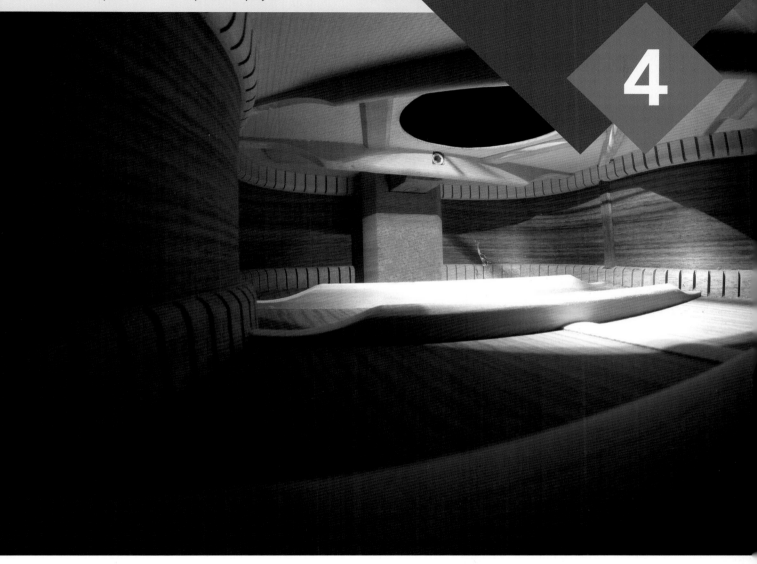

START SPEAKING

A   How would you describe this picture? Which adjectives from the box would you use? What other words can you think of? Do you like it? Why or why not? Can you guess what it shows? (Answer is at the bottom of the page.)

| elegant | impressive | modern | striking | stunning | unusual | weird |

B   When you're too concerned with the details of something, people say, "You can't see the forest for the trees." Do you have a similar expression in your language? Can you think of an example of a time when you couldn't see the forest because there were too many trees? For ideas, watch Audrey's video.

EXPERT SPEAKER

What kinds of things might Audrey call "trees," and what's her "forest"?

Answer: The inside of a guitar.

UNDER THE MICROSCOPE

1 LANGUAGE IN CONTEXT

TAKING A **CLOSER LOOK**

Microphotography is the perfect blend of art and science. It shows us everyday objects, most of which we ignore at normal size, in all their magnified beauty.

A _____

B _____

C _____

A 🔊 **1.30** **Read the introduction to a podcast. What is microphotography? Look at the pictures. What do you think they show? Listen to the podcast and label the pictures. Were you right?**

🔊 **1.30 Audio script**

Have you ever let a handful of sand run through your fingers and wondered what each tiny grain might look like close up? Gary Greenberg did. Greenberg is a medical scientist and microphotographer. He collected sand from all over the world, magnified each sample to 250 times its usual size, and revealed a **miniature**, **multicolored** wonderland. The images show grains of sand, each of which is totally unique, to be **circular**, **spiral**, and **cylindrical** particles with textures from silky smooth to **ridged** and rough.

Microphotographers, many of whom are primarily scientists, remake the tiniest pieces of the world around us in **mammoth** size. Pollen, which we usually only notice when it makes us sneeze, looks like a handful of fruity candy. Household dust becomes an **elaborate** assortment of **stringy** fibers, **flaky** discs of dried skin, and micro-drops of cosmetics.

But it isn't all abstract art from the **filthy** floor. Microphotography has practical applications for many branches of science. In medicine, it allows doctors to study the **delicate** structures of viruses that previously they knew very little about. In marine biology, researchers use the technique to track the growth and spread of microplastics in our oceans.

Microphotography offers a fresh outlook on the world we live in, helping us appreciate all that we cannot see.

B 🔊 **1.30** | PAIR WORK | THINK CRITICALLY | **Listen again. What two practical uses of microphotography are mentioned? What other practical uses can you think of?**

GLOSSARY
fibers (*n, pl*) long pieces that combine to make fabric
particle (*n*) a very small piece of something

2 VOCABULARY: Describing things

FIND IT

A 🔊 **1.31** **Look at the bold words in the audio script. Can you figure out their meaning from context and the pictures? Write them in the correct category in the chart below. You can use a dictionary or your phone to help you. Listen and check.**

Describing size	Describing shape	Describing qualities
miniature	circular	multicolored

B ▶ **Now go to page 144. Do the vocabulary exercises for 4.1.**

C   PAIR WORK   THINK CRITICALLY   Find a small object in the classroom, your pockets, your clothing or jewelry, or your bag. Look at it closely and note its size, shape, and particular qualities. Describe it to your partner. Can they guess what it is, based on your description?

> It's **cylindrical** and very thin. It's kind of **delicate** but not very **elaborate**.

> Oh, I know! It's your earring.

3   GRAMMAR: Quantifiers and prepositions in relative clauses

A   **Read the sentences in the grammar box. Then complete the rules with words from the box.**

Quantifiers and prepositions in relative clauses

It shows us everyday objects, **most of which** we ignore at normal size.

The images show grains of sand, **each of which** is totally unique.

Microphotographers, **many of whom** are scientists, remake the tiniest pieces of the world around us.

Pollen, **which we usually only notice** when it makes us sneeze, looks like a handful of fruit candy.

It allows doctors to study the structures of viruses **that previously they knew very little about**.

after	each	many	things	whom

We can use quantifiers such as *all of*, [1]_____ *of*, [2]_____ *of*, *most of*, *much of*, *none of*, and *some of* with the relative pronouns *which* and [3]_____ at the beginning of a relative clause. Use *which* for [4]_____ and *whom* for people.

Except in very formal written texts, prepositions in relative clauses come [5]_____ the verb.

B   ▶   **Now go to page 132. Look at the grammar chart and do the grammar exercise for 4.1.**

C   PAIR WORK   **Read the statements and look at the bold phrases. Correct those that are wrong, and reorder the words in those that are unnecessarily formal. Are any of the sentences true for you? In what way?**

1   I have a lot of good friends, **many of which** I've known since kindergarten.
2   My teachers give us a lot of tests, **most of whom** I pass easily.
3   I subscribe to about 12 different podcasts, **to which I listen** during my commute.
4   I'm working with a new person **about whom I know very little**.

4   SPEAKING

A   GROUP WORK   **Look at the extreme close-ups. What do you think they show? Why? (Answers are at the bottom of page 42.)**

B   **Which picture do you find the most interesting? The most beautiful? The most bizarre? How would you describe each image without saying what it is?**

> This one is a microphotograph of different fibers, **some of which** are very **stringy**.

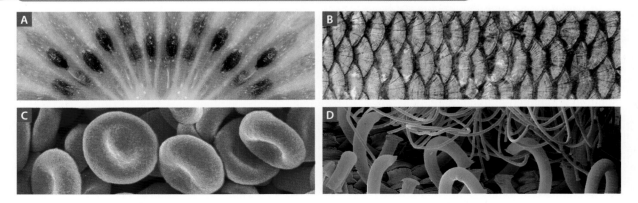

EYE TO EYE

1 LANGUAGE IN CONTEXT

A   Read about the human eye. Check (✓) the information you already knew. Write *!* for information that surprises you and *?* for facts you'd like to learn more about.

SIX THINGS YOU DIDN'T KNOW ABOUT THE HUMAN EYE

The human eye is an incredible organ, second only to the brain in its complexity. Here are a few amazing facts about what our eyes can do and how they do it.

____ 1 Our eyes don't grow. That's why a baby's eyes look so big. Their size is the same as adult eyes, though eyesight won't develop fully until about one year of age.

____ 2 We blink an average of 20 times per minute. That's more than 4 million times a year!

____ 3 Our eyes can process 10 million different colors – but only when there's light! Without light, colors fade, and what we see is a world of grays.

____ 4 We focus and refocus on different objects, details, and distances literally in the blink of an eye. For a camera to equal how well the human eye perceives detail, it would need a resolution of more than 500 megapixels.

____ 5 Every eye is unique because of the patterns and colors of the iris. Greek physician Hippocrates first noticed this in 390 BCE. Today, security agencies use iris scanning to confirm that we are who we say we are.

____ 6 Blind people who have never had vision dream in colors and images. There's no real way, however, to know if the images in their mind's eye look like things in the real world.

FIND IT

B   PAIR WORK   Compare your responses. Did your partner know things that you didn't? Go online to find out more about your "?" items. Share the information with other students.

FIND IT

2 VOCABULARY: Eye idioms and metaphors

A   🔊 1.32   PAIR WORK   Listen to the expressions in the box. Which were used in the article? What do you think each one means? In what situation might you use it? You can use a dictionary or your phone to help you.

a bird's eye view of	catch your eye	feast your eyes on	in the public eye
in the blink of an eye	in your mind's eye	keep your eyes on the prize	see eye to eye on
turn a blind eye to	without batting an eye	have eyes in the back of your head	

B   ▶ Now go to page 144. Do the vocabulary exercises for 4.2.

C   GROUP WORK   Discuss the questions.
- Share your answers from exercise 2A. Do you all agree on the meaning of the different expressions? What situations did you come up with for using them?
- What idioms and metaphors about eyes and vision are in your language? How would you translate them to English? Are any of them similar to the ones presented in this lesson?

3 GRAMMAR: Noun clauses with question words

A Read the sentences in the grammar box. <u>Underline</u> the question words in the **bold** phrases. Then complete the rules below with words from the box.

> ### Noun clauses with question words
>
> Here are a few amazing facts about **what our eyes can do** and **how they do it**.
>
> Without light, colors fade, and **what we see** is a world of grays.
>
> Today, security agencies use iris scanning to confirm we are **who we say we are**.

how	prepositions	questions	statement	subject	what	who

Question words can be substituted for general nouns. For example, ¹_____ can be used for *the thing/things*, ²_____ for *the person/people*, or ³_____ for *the way*.

We can use this type of noun clause as both the ⁴_____ and object of the verb and also with ⁵_____ . These clauses use question words, but they are not ⁶_____ . The word order is the same as in a ⁷_____ .

B ▶ Now go to page 132. Look at the grammar chart and do the grammar exercise for 4.2.

C (Circle) the correct question word for the categories. Add two more categories of your own.

1 *what / where / how* I can see from the window in my room
2 *which / how / who* I get to work/school every day and *when / which / what* I see on the way
3 *what / which / why* I'm studying English and *what / how / where* I see it affecting my life
4 _____
5 _____

D PAIR WORK Write example sentences for the categories in exercise 3C and check your accuracy. Then read one of your sentences to a partner. Can your partner guess the category? Read another.

4 SPEAKING

A GROUP WORK Discuss the questions.

- Do you think it's important to see eye to eye on everything with your friends? With your family?

- Are you easily distracted or discouraged, or do you always keep your eyes on the prize?

- When you were little, what were your parents strict about, and what did they turn a blind eye to? Did your parents seem to have eyes in the back of their heads? For ideas, watch Audrey's video.

EXPERT SPEAKER

In what ways were your parents like Audrey's?

> ✓ **ACCURACY** CHECK
>
> Don't add the auxiliary verbs *do* or *did* in noun clauses with question words.
>
> *What ~~do~~ we see is a world of grays.* ✗
> *What we see is a world of grays.* ✓

> *Seeing eye to eye* with your family is nice, but it isn't necessary.

B Look at the picture to the right. Which animal does this eye belong to? How are the eyes of this animal different from human eyes?

4.3 LOOK AWAY!

1 LISTENING

A **PAIR WORK** What types of screens do you look at for work or For pleasure? About how many hours a day do you spend a screen? What effect might this be having on your eyes?

B 🔊 **1.33** **LISTEN FOR MAIN IDEA** Listen to an ophthalmologist (eye doctor) discussing the effect of screens on our eyes. Which statement best summarizes her position?

   a Screen viewing causes serious and lasting damage to our eyes.

   b There is no need to cut back on the amount of time we spend looking at screens.

   c We can take a number of practical steps to help protect our eyesight.

C 🔊 **1.33** **LISTEN FOR DETAILS** Listen again and pay attention to the structure of the presentation. Use the chart to take notes.

	How and why this affects eyesight	Proposed solution(s)
Blinking		
Glare and reflections		
Blue light		

D **PAIR WORK** Compare your notes. Did you capture all the same information? Was it presented in an organized way? Do you think the ophthalmologist offers good advice? Do you do any of these things? Will you do any of them now?

INSIDER ENGLISH

Easier said than done. = It's not as easy as it seems.

2 PRONUNCIATION: Listening for /t/ between vowels

A 🔊 **1.34** Listen to the two sets of phrases. In which set are the <u>underlined</u> /t/ sounds pronounced more like /d/?

   a But the truth of the ma<u>tt</u>er is …   **b** … there are lots of prac<u>t</u>ical things …

      It's a vi<u>t</u>al function for healthy eyes …   … special yellow-<u>t</u>inted glasses …

B 🔊 **1.35** **PAIR WORK** <u>Underline</u> the /t/ sounds that might sound more like /d/ sounds. Listen and check. Then practice saying the sentences with a partner.

   1 We've invited ophthalmologist Kit Bradley to the studio today …

   2 This constant fatigue leads to eyestrain with all its related problems.

   3 Blue light is emitted by digital screens.

C (Circle) the correct words to complete the sentence.

The /t/ sound is often pronounced more like /d/ when it comes after ¹*a stressed / an unstressed* vowel and before ²*a stressed / an unstressed* vowel.

3 SPEAKING SKILLS

A 🔊 **1.33** PAIR WORK **Complete the sentences from the interview. Listen to the interview again to check your answers. Do any of the bold words have a /t/ sound that is more like a /d/ sound? Underline them.**

> ### Clarifying a problem
>
> 1   It's not quite that **straightforward** when you look at it more _____.
> 2   That's the **key to** finding a _____.
> 3   That has a **major impact** on …
> 4   **There's** _____ **more to it** than just blinking.
> 5   The **truth of the matter** is, …
> 6   This **gets to the** _____ **of** the problem.
> 7   Blue light isn't a _____ thing **in itself**.
> 8   It all **comes down to** how much blue light our eyes are exposed to.
> 9   _____ at it **objectively**, …

B PAIR WORK **Look at the expressions in the chart again. What do the bold words and phrases mean? Which word or phrase from the box below could replace each one?**

> big effect   depends on   highlights the basis of
> necessarily   realistically   it's much more complicated
> reality   simple   most important information for

C PAIR WORK **Using your notes from exercise 1C on page 38 and expressions from the chart in exercise 3A, write an organized summary of the problems that can result from spending too much time looking at screens. Read your summary to another pair of students and listen to their feedback. Revise your summary.**

4 PRONUNCIATION: Saying the stressed syllable in related words

A 🔊 **1.36** **Listen to the difference in stress in the related words.**

1   objectively   an object   to object   3   complicated   complication
2   photography   photograph   photographic

B 🔊 **1.37** **Listen and underline the stressed syllables. Then repeat all the words.**

1   microscope   microphotography   3   primary   primarily   5   to substitute   substitution
2   to magnify   magnificent   4   technique   technical   6   impact   to impact

C PAIR WORK **Choose a set of words from exercise 4B and point to it for your partner. Hum the syllable stress of one of the two words in the set. Can your partner tell which word it is? Reverse roles and do it again.**

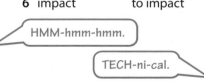

HMM-hmm-hmm.

TECH-ni-cal.

5 SPEAKING

A PAIR WORK **Discuss the connections that might exist between screen time and the topics in the box. Can you think of any other areas that might be affected?**

> back pain   general health   poor posture   screen addiction   sleep problems

B PAIR WORK **Choose two or three of the topics you talked about and discuss possible solutions. Organize your ideas into a short presentation. Look again at the chart in exercise 1C to help you.**

C **Share your solutions with the class. Describe the main factors you took into consideration.**

4.4 ATTENTION TO DETAIL

LESSON OBJECTIVE
- write a personal profile statement for a résumé

1 READING

A **PAIR WORK** How would you answer the question in the quiz? Which answer options reflect big-picture thinking? Which focus on details? Read the article to check your answers. Are you a big-picture thinker or more detail oriented?

DETAILS OR THE BIG PICTURE
– WHERE IS YOUR FOCUS?

Question 1 When you meet a person for the first time, which of the following are you likely to notice?

- Their mood
- Their shoes
- Whether they make eye contact
- The fact that they have a coffee stain on their shirt

BIG-PICTURE VS. DETAIL-ORIENTED: HOW DO YOU THINK?

Are you a big-picture thinker who focuses on the main issues but misses some of the important details? Or are you detail oriented, able to see all the parts but not quite able to see the whole? Find out more about the two mindsets.

Big-picture thinkers

Big-picture thinkers look at things from a global perspective. They grasp a situation in the blink of an eye, identify the main problem, and see what needs to be done to resolve it. They are great motivators and often make inspirational leaders. Their coworkers, friends, and family know that they can trust their judgement.

In the business world, big-picture people spot opportunities that others might miss. They are strategic planners, leading their companies from the front, providing the momentum for change and innovation. In fields of science, they push beyond current knowledge and make huge breakthroughs. In an academic context, they are the students who make connections, who see patterns in the shifts and turns of history or economics, who understand the wider significance of phenomena in biology or chemistry.

Awareness of the big picture, the desire to capture and share it, and an ability to communicate it is what has led to mankind's greatest inventions.

Detail-oriented people

Detail-oriented people have a different mindset. They do not lack imagination or inspiration, but they are observant and analytical. They notice everything and foresee difficulties before they become problems. When a problem arises, they break it down into its component parts, resolving each issue to form a complete solution. Nothing escapes their meticulous attention and their eye for detail.

Detail-oriented people are the backbone of any successful business. They make sure the grand plans can be achieved. They dedicate time and energy to checking and rechecking each step and making sure that nothing endangers success. Their support and diligence provide the team with a sense of security and confidence. In science, they are the tireless researchers whose painstaking work makes sure the big theories have a sound, practical basis. In an academic context, they are the students who know their subject matter inside and out.

The best of both worlds

It's tempting to value one mindset over the other, but the truth is that both big-picture and detail-oriented mindsets are necessary to the success of any enterprise. Fortunately, hardly anybody is exclusively one or the other. We all tend to show qualities of both mindsets, though we also usually lean towards just one. Knowing which way you lean is key to choosing coworkers, friends, and life partners whose strengths will complement yours.

B **READ FOR MAIN IDEA** Which single sentence best summarizes the whole article? Underline it.

C **PAIR WORK** **READ FOR DETAILS** Write *B* for words associated with big-picture thinkers or *D* for qualities of detail-oriented people. Find the expressions in the article and check your answers.

1 diligence D
2 inspirational leaders ___
3 meticulous attention ___
4 painstaking work ___
5 strategic planners ___
6 tireless researchers ___

D **PAIR WORK** **THINK CRITICALLY** Discuss the questions.

- The article focuses on advantages. What are some possible disadvantages of each perspective?
- What kinds of careers would be better suited to big-picture thinkers and detail-oriented people? Why?

40

2 WRITING

A **Read the profile statements. What kind of job is each person looking for? Which people seem to be more detailed oriented, and which seem to be more focused on the big picture?**

A

I have a clear, logical mind **with a practical approach to problem-solving** and a strong drive to see things through to completion. **As a graduate with a double major in marketing and business**, I am eager to put my degree to good use and apply the principles I have learned to actual business ventures.

B

A seasoned professional **with a successful track record** and strong technical skills, I approach each project **with a keen eye for detail**. I am eager to be challenged in order to improve my IT skills and grow professionally.

REGISTER CHECK

When writing about yourself in formal contexts, be careful not to start every sentence with the personal pronoun *I*.

C

From the corporate world to dot com startups, my abilities at team management have been tested and proven. **With resourceful problem-solving techniques and an optimistic outlook on life**, I excel at motivating others to do their best work.

B **CREATE COHESION** **Look at the bold phrases in the profile statements in exercise 2A. They all start with a preposition. Rewrite them as full sentences, making all other changes necessary.**

I have a clear, logical mind. I like to follow a practical approach to solving problems. I have a strong drive to see things through to completion as a result.

C **PAIR WORK** **Combine the sentences to make the profile statement below more concise. Compare statements with a partner. Did you make the same changes?**

I am an experienced construction foreman. I have had experience with everything from houses to skyscrapers. My greatest strengths are scheduling, budgeting, and anticipating problems. I have proven that I can bring projects to completion on time and on budget. Some of the largest construction firms in the area have entrusted me with their projects. Some of them were their most sensitive projects.

 **WRITE IT**

D **PLAN** **You're going to write a personal profile statement for job candidate new to their career. First, with a partner, discuss the jobs in the box below. What qualities are needed for each job? How might a candidate address them?**

elementary school teacher   project manager   research assistant

E **Choose one of the jobs and write the candidate's statement on your own. Be sure to combine related ideas to make it concise.**

F **PAIR WORK** **Read your statements to each other. Offer feedback for improvement.**

G **PAIR WORK** **After a few years in the job, your candidates are now looking for a change. Choose a new career and rewrite the previous statement to incorporate the candidate's experience and how that would address the qualities that the new job would require.**

elementary school teacher   hotel manager
medical lab technician   project manager
research assistant   youth club coordinator

TIME TO SPEAK
Every last detail

A **PREPARE** With a partner, look at the poster. What kind of convention or event do you think it might be? Make a list of possibilities. Which of them would you be most interested in attending? Choose one of your ideas and brainstorm activities that would probably take place. Use the prompts to help you.

demonstrations	exhibitions	film screenings
performances	presentations	social events

We proudly present the 15th annual

CLOSE UP

FRIDAY, MAY 15, TO SUNDAY, MAY 17

The Marionette Suite, Plaza Hotel

www.closeupcon.com ▶

B **DISCUSS** You are the organizers. Think about the things you need to do to prepare for the convention or event. Start with the big-picture categories like those below. What other categories can you think of?

brochure

catering / food service

guest speakers / performers

promotion / advertising

social events

target audience

venue

_____

_____

_____

C **DECIDE** Work with another pair of students to create an action plan. Follow the steps.

Step 1 Make a list of what needs to be done in each category.

Step 2 Prioritize the lists.

Step 3 Decide when each action needs to be completed and how much time it will require.

Step 4 Choose who in your group is responsible for which lists and/or actions.

Step 5 Make a detailed plan of action. Consider which tasks or lists can be done independently and which ones affect other people's work.

D **PRESENT** Present an overview of your convention or event to the class and then break it down into your action plan. Listen to the other groups. Ask and answer questions.

E **AGREE** What did you learn from this experience? Discuss the questions.

■ Which people are better at big-picture tasks? Who is more detail oriented? What about your own strengths?

■ Did your group have a good mix of people in it, or were your strengths unbalanced? Do you think this affected your plan positively or negatively? Why? If you did this project again, would you assign tasks differently?

■ Considering all the plans presented, which convention or event would you most want to attend? Why?

To check your progress, go to page 154.

USEFUL PHRASES

DISCUSS

For the venue, we'll need to consider … in our decision.

Before we choose … , let's decide …

Figuring out … will help us determine …

DECIDE

For … , it all comes down to …

In this category, the highest priorities are …

Once you've done … , I can start …

Answers to exercise 4A, page 35: A a slice of kiwi, B salmon scales, C human red blood cells, D Velcro fastener

UNIT OBJECTIVES

- discuss traveling to remote places
- comment on loneliness and working in remote places
- discuss cause and effect
- write a company profile
- prepare and present a case for working remotely

REMOTE

5

START SPEAKING

A   Look at the picture. Where do you think this is? Do you think the building is a home? Why or why not? How does the idea of being in this place make you feel?

B   What would be the challenges of living in a place like this? Think of the type of person who would choose to live here. What physical or mental characteristics do you think they might have?

C   What movies, books, shows, or real-life stories do you know in which people live in some type of isolation? How do they handle it? Is isolation a choice or an accident? For ideas, watch Susanne's video.

EXPERT SPEAKER

Do you agree with Susanne's conclusions?

5.1

THE END OF
THE ROAD

LESSON OBJECTIVE
- discuss traveling to
  remote places

1 LANGUAGE IN CONTEXT

A   **Look at the pictures and the title of the article. What do you think "Project Remote" is? Read and check
your prediction.**

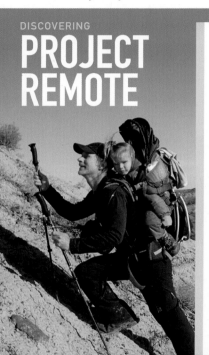

DISCOVERING
PROJECT REMOTE

Walking down a crowded, noisy beach one day in
Florida, Ryan and Rebecca Means suddenly looked at
each other and had the same thought: Let's find a place
that is just the opposite of this. They didn't want just a
deserted or unpopulated area, they wanted to find a
place that nobody had ever visited!

And so Project Remote was born. Their first mission was
to find the most remote place in their state. But having
explored all the spots close to home, they soon found
themselves itching for more. Analyzing satellite imagery,
Rebecca identified the places in the U.S. that are farthest
away from human structures. Now addicted to the beauty of **unspoiled** landscapes, they drove
from state to state, visiting the most isolated places imaginable, and they brought their toddler,
Skyla, along.

Searching out the most remote spots sometimes ended in disappointment. They would arrive
and find other people had beaten them there or a new road had just been built nearby!

The Means family's favorite places are the **immense**, **nameless** expanses of the West. The most
remote spot they have found so far is deep in Yellowstone National Park in Wyoming.

Described in great detail on their blog Project Remote, the family's routes form a **scenic** memoir
of their adventures, and their photos bring it all to life: from the **lush** green swamplands of
Florida to the **bare**, **hostile** deserts of Arizona. Log on and enjoy the remoteness!

B   **PAIR WORK** **THINK CRITICALLY** **What is Project Remote's mission? Would you like to go on one of their trips?
Why or why not? In what ways do you think Project Remote's work could be beneficial to society?**

2 VOCABULARY: Describing remote places

A   🔊 **1.38** **Look at the bold adjectives in the article in exercise 1A. Match them to the synonyms below. More than
one match is possible. Then listen to check your work.**

1	isolated	_____	5	anonymous	_____
2	barren	_____	6	picturesque	_____
3	vast	_____	7	abandoned	_____
4	abundant	_____	8	harsh	_____

FIND IT

B   **Which adjectives are usually used to describe places in a positive way? In a negative way? Which are neutral?
Use a dictionary or your phone to help you. Then use your phone to find more examples of these words
in context.**

C   ▶ **Now go to page 145. Do the vocabulary exercises for 5.1.**

D   **PAIR WORK** **THINK CRITICALLY** **Think of a landscape near you. Which adjectives would apply to it?
Describe it in detail.**

> The beaches are really **unspoiled** and **scenic**, but they are not
> **deserted**. They're really popular with families in the summer.

3 GRAMMAR: Participle phrases in initial position

A Read the sentences in the grammar box. (Circle) the correct options to complete the rules.

> **Participle phrases in initial position**
>
> **Walking down a crowded, noisy beach**, they looked at each other and had the same thought.
> **Having explored all the spots close to home**, they found themselves itching for more.
> **Now addicted to the beauty of unspoiled landscapes**, they drove from state to state.

1 Participle phrases at the beginning of a sentence **contain / don't contain** a subject.

2 The subject of the verb in the participle phrase **is the same as / is different from** the subject of the verb in the main clause.

3 There **is only one type / are different types** of participles. A participle phrase can start with **only one / any** of them.

B ➤ **Now go to page 133. Look at the grammar chart and do the grammar exercise for 5.1.**

C PAIR WORK Using participle phrases and the prompts below, write sentences that are true for you. Read them to your partner. Then check your accuracy.

1 look at social media / feel connected

2 study English / understand movies and TV shows

3 strict parents / be strict to own children

4 travel to unfamiliar places / chance to explore / people and cultures

> Looking at my family's posts on social media, I feel connected to them, even though they're far away.

ACCURACY CHECK

Don't use *to* + verb in participle clauses.

Finally having ~~to find~~ the right path, we reached the lake in no time. ✗
Finally having found the right path, we reached the lake in no time. ✓

4 SPEAKING

A PAIR WORK THINK CRITICALLY If you wanted to get away and be by yourself for a week, which type of place would appeal to you more? Why?

- a bare environment, like a vast expanse of hostile, barren desert
- a lush, scenic jungle, with picturesque views and abundant life, but no people
- a boat floating along in some immense, anonymous part of the ocean

> Having lived my whole life in a lush, green area, I think I'd choose the ocean. The weather can be **harsh** at times, but the **vast** emptiness of it appeals to me.

HOW TO BE ALONE

1 LANGUAGE IN CONTEXT

A 🔊 **1.39** Look at the picture on page 47. What is the man doing? Listen to a podcast about two people's jobs and check your answers. Which job is related to the picture?

🔊 1.39 Audio script

Host	Today, we'll learn about two people who live and work alone in remote locations. What **impact** has constant solitude had on them? What **implications** might it have for their futures? Susan, who lives and works on an island, is our first guest.
Susan	My job is to guard the archeological sites here. A few researchers come sometimes, but no tourists. I can see how someone freaked out by solitude would find this job impossible, but people have always been a **source** of anxiety for me, so I'm fine. The quiet helps me think. I've even started writing again. I see solitude as a positive **force** in my life. As a **consequence**, I'm kind of addicted to it.
Host	Next we hear from Austin, who is a fire officer in an area of the Rocky Mountains known to be extremely difficult to reach. Solitude has **influenced** him very differently.
Austin	Wildfires, common during the summer season, can happen really anytime, so five times a day I climb the lookout tower. When I see smoke, I send a signal that **triggers** firefighters to investigate. A few friends have visited me, but I couldn't really talk to them, which probably **stems from** the fact that I hardly talk at all anymore. But that **resulted in** even fewer visitors and more solitude. I want to be around people again. This experience has even **motivated** me to apply to grad school, to study communications!

B **THINK CRITICALLY** Is either of the people in the podcast lonely? What would you say is the difference between loneliness and solitude? Does one always trigger the other? Is it possible to feel lonely when you're not alone? Why or why not?

2 VOCABULARY: Talking about influences

A 🔊 **1.40** **PAIR WORK** Look at the **bold** words in the audio script. Try to work out what they mean from context. Then make a chart like the one below and write them in the correct category according to how they're used in the text. Listen and check.

Nouns	Verbs
impact	influence

B ▶ Now go to page 145. Do the vocabulary exercises for 5.2.

C **PAIR WORK** | **THINK CRITICALLY** Think of a problem that you have personal experience with. Discuss your ideas about its source(s), how it influences your life, and what implications it might have for your future.

> I'm always late, and it has a really negative **impact** on my life. My friends get mad because we always miss the beginning of the movie. As a **consequence**, they don't invite me to things anymore.

> What do you think this habit **stems** from?

3 GRAMMAR: Reduced relative clauses

A **Read the sentences in the grammar box. Complete the rules.**

> ### Reduced relative clauses
>
> I can see how **someone (who is)** freaked out by solitude would find this job impossible.
>
> **Wildfires, (which are)** common during the summer season, can happen anytime.
>
> It is an area **(that is)** known to be extremely difficult to reach.

1 A relative clause consists of a relative pronoun (*which*, _____ , or *that*) and a verb phrase.

2 When the verb phrase starts with the verb *be*, we can drop both the _____ _____ and *be*.

B ▶ **Now go to page 133. Look at the grammar chart and do the grammar exercise for 5.2.**

C PAIR WORK **Combine the two sentences using a complete relative clause. Then** ~~cross out~~ **two words to form a reduced relative clause. Compare your work with a partner. What is your opinion about each statement?**

1 Some people are not used to being alone. They probably shouldn't work as freelancers.

   ~~People who are~~ not used to being alone probably shouldn't work as freelancers.

2 Some students enroll in distance learning programs. They attend class via a conferencing app.

   _____

3 Some people are willing to work in solitude for long periods. They are hard to find.

   _____

4 Language learning is known to be easier for children. It is a common retirement goal for adults.

   _____

4 SPEAKING

A GROUP WORK THINK CRITICALLY **Discuss the questions.**

■ What's the difference between solitude and loneliness?

■ What are some consequences of having too much or too little solitude as a child?

■ What impact does solitude have on you? Is it a positive, creative force in your life, or is it a source of anxiety?

> I'm not someone **afraid of being alone**. Solitude is a **source** of relaxation for me.

B PAIR WORK **Can you think of jobs in which people work alone? Is it by choice or by necessity? What might motivate someone to choose these jobs? Would you like to do any of them? Why or why not? For ideas, watch Susanne's video.**

EXPERT
SPEAKER

How similar are you and Susanne?

5.3 WORKING FROM HOME

1 LISTENING

A 🔊 **1.41** **PAIR WORK** Look at the pictures. In which context would you prefer to work? Why? What are some pros and cons for each context? Listen to a presentation about working remotely. Does the speaker mention any of your points?

B 🔊 **1.41** **DIFFERENTIATE FACTS AND OPINIONS** Read the excerpts from the presentation and write *O* (opinion) or *F* (fact). Listen to the presentation again. What difference in tone do you hear?

1   … we all know that's due to the digital revolution. ___

2   … the productivity of remote workers was ranked as 7.7 out of 10, compared with 6.5 out of 10 for office workers. ___

3   This must be thanks to the reduction in distractions that people have at home … ___

4   … another study found that those who spent 60 to 80 percent of their time away from the office had the highest rates of engagement with their coworkers. ___

5   … remote workers are more likely to report that their coworkers care about them as a person and as a professional. ___

6   What's important is the autonomy of working where I like, instead of where someone else puts me. ___

INSIDER ENGLISH

Say *As it turns out* to indicate an unexpected result or circumstance.

I thought I'd hate working in a big office, but as it turns out, I find it really energizing.

C 🔊 **1.41** **LISTEN FOR ORGANIZATION** Listen to the presentation again. How does the speaker start? How does she introduce the topic? How does she wrap up her talk?

D **PAIR WORK** **THINK CRITICALLY** Do you share the presenter's opinion about remote work? Why or why not? Which specific points do you disagree with? Would you say the presentation accurately reflects the experience of working remotely?

2 PRONUNCIATION: Listening for linking between words

A 🔊 **1.42** Listen to the phrases and notice how some words are linked. What sounds are they?

a   … according to a survey of …

b   Commuting is a major source of stress.

c   … as readily as others.

d   For all the reasons I've presented, …

B 🔊 **1.43** **PAIR WORK** Underline where linking sounds will occur between the words below. Listen and check.

When a word ends with a consonant sound and the next word starts with a vowel sound, the two words are usually

linked together if they are in the same word group. When a word ends with a vowel sound and the next

word begins with a vowel sound, there is usually also a linking sound.

C Circle the correct words to complete the sentences.

If the first word ends in a vowel where the lips are [1]*rounded / spread*, for example /i/, there is a linking sound like /j/.
If the first word ends in a vowel where the lips are [2]*rounded / spread*, for example /u/, there is a linking sound like /w/.
But if the first word ends in /r/, /a/, or /ɜ/, then /j/, /w/, and /r/ link to the next word.

3 SPEAKING SKILLS

A 🔊 **1.44** Listen again and complete the phrases from the presentation. What linking sounds do you hear?

> **Signaling cause and effect**
>
> 1 More and more people are working from home, and we all know that's ___due to___ the digital revolution.   *C*
>
> 2 _____ studies found lower stress levels among remote workers, _____ a reduction in their chance of suffering heart attacks and strokes.   ___
>
> 3 This must be _____ the reduction in distractions that people have at home.   ___
>
> 4 _____ the added flexibility that remote working allows, the gender gap is reduced.   ___
>
> 5 A common _____ of working from home is loneliness.   ___
>
> 6 _____ I've presented, remote work should no longer be just regarded as a job "perk."   ___
>
> 7 As an employee, _____ I have more power over the way I do my work, I'm happier, and I get more done.   ___

B **PAIR WORK** Look at the sentences in the chart again. Write *C* for expressions that signal a cause and *E* for those that signal an effect. Compare with a partner.

C **PAIR WORK** Student A reads the statement below. Student B responds using a cause-and-effect expression. Take turns and continue with statements of your own.

>   **Statement:** I don't like the idea of working from home.

> That's because you're very sociable. But I find that I get so much more done when I'm working from home.

> Thanks to the peace and quiet, I suppose.

> **REGISTER** CHECK
>
> The most formal cause-and-effect expressions are usually only found in written contexts:
>
> as a result of   thus   owing to
>
> consequently   the consequences of

4 PRONUNCIATION: Saying tense and lax vowels

A 🔊 **1.45** Listen and repeat. Are the <u>underlined</u> vowels tense or lax? Write *T* or *L*.

1 dig<u>i</u>tal L	3 p<u>eo</u>ple ___	5 red<u>u</u>ce ___	7 reg<u>a</u>rded ___
2 employ<u>ee</u> ___	4 p<u>er</u>k ___	6 red<u>u</u>ction ___	8 g<u>a</u>p ___

B 🔊 **1.46** **PAIR WORK** Read the words aloud and (circle) all the lax vowels you hear. Listen and check.

1 arch(i)tect	3 employee	5 perk	7 remote
2 digital	4 manager	6 real estate	8 stress

C **PAIR WORK** Make your own list of words containing tense and lax vowels. Quiz your partner.

5 SPEAKING

A **PAIR WORK** **THINK CRITICALLY** Choose one of the topics in the box or another topic that you both know something about. Prepare a mini-presentation (2–5 minutes) about the pros and cons associated with it. Look at exercise 1C to help you. Be sure to use phrases for cause and effect. Ask and answer questions to improve your work.

> social media   tech devices   vegetarianism   video games

B Give your mini-presentation to the class. How many different topics were presented?

> Our topic is tech devices. People have a lot more options for working today thanks to the internet and Wi-Fi, but mostly because of great tech devices.

> But in some ways, technology also limits our choices. As a result of the internet, some industries are dying. . . .

REMOTE SUCCESS STORY

1 READING

A **PREDICT CONTENT** Look at the title of the article and the picture. What do you think the story is about?

B **READ FOR MAIN IDEA** Read the article and choose the best summary of it.

a A company that people have never heard of can be very important to modern life.

b One company has managed to embrace new ways of working successfully.

c A remote company can best compete with its more traditional business rivals.

BUSINESS Home　Fortune 100　News　Search

Automattic goes fully remote

Automattic – the company behind thousands of blogs and open-source platforms – has closed its gorgeous San Francisco office because their employees never show up. And that's a sign of the times!

Best known for giving the world the free blogging platform WordPress, Automattic powers 20 percent of all websites on the internet today – a staggering figure.

As a result of their success, you might imagine them overseeing their empire from a huge, multi-million-dollar building in a trendy but expensive neighborhood, but you'd be wrong. While they do have an office, it's small, cozy, inexpensive, and now nearly empty.

Thanks to the wonders of modern technology, Automattic's vast web empire is managed completely online. This enables their team of 400 employees distributed across 40 countries to work seamlessly without sharing an office, or perhaps even more amazingly, without using email.

How can they work this way? The secret, ironically, is total transparency. Everybody knows exactly what's going on. All meetings, even those that happen with people in the same location, take place online. Consequently, everyone has equal status and stays in the loop. Day-to-day communication is done through internal blogs hosted on WordPress, the business communication app Slack, and the occasional video chat.

The company provides and maintains all the tools and software an employee needs to work remotely; thus, all employees have access to the same platforms and work in compatible programs. If a home office is the preferred location, the company pays for an ergonomic consultation to ensure a healthy work environment, even remotely. For those who choose to seek out a coworking space, Automattic pays the costs associated with it, including their cappuccino at a coffee shop if that's where employees choose to set up camp.

Automattic has found that remote working helps them attract top talent: not just locals, but also people who don't live in San Francisco or can't live there, owing to that city's famously high rents. But the company saves money, too. They declined to say how much of the savings was due to the office closure, but ditching a 15,000-square-foot office space in San Francisco would have to make a difference to any company's bottom line.

Regardless of where the increased profits come from, Automattic shares the bounty with their employees. Consider "hack week": Automattic will pay for any team to meet in person and work for one week in any location in the world. Now, that can't be bad!

GLOSSARY

in the loop (*phr*) in possession of all current and relevant information needed

C **READ FOR DETAILS** Find six examples of cause-and-effect expressions in the article. What alternatives might you use if you were telling a friend the same information?

D **PAIR WORK** **THINK CRITICALLY** Discuss the questions.

1 What would you say is the writer's attitude toward Automattic and their decision to go remote? Find examples to defend your opinion.

2 What do you think Automattic's main motivation is – cutting costs, helping their workers, or something else? Why do you think so?

2 WRITING

A Read this profile about another remote firm called "The Company." What are the five main factors they point to for their success?

100% VIRTUAL?

The Company, interested for years in remote business models, has gone 100% virtual. Here, we explain the strategies behind their distributed workforce.

First, The Company hired the right employees. Millennials, already accustomed to working remotely, are the key. Location and time spent on work have always been flexible for them, so they adapt well to working virtually.

Another strategy is to be proactive about communication. Meetings held via video chats are replacing traditional messaging methods. They have found this practice also makes it easier to keep everybody in the loop.

Then there's flexibility around working hours. Employees, happy with their own customized schedules, work far more efficiently. Flexible hours also reduce employee stress.

The next challenge was learning how to manage effectively via technology. Thanks to virtual office software now available, managers at The Company don't have to worry about not being able to monitor what employees are doing. Managers and coworkers can always see when team members are working or available to chat, giving everyone a sense of teamwork.

Finally, The Company never forgets the value of face time. Even if it's only once a year, they look for opportunities for teams to meet in person and work side by side.

B **CREATE COHESION** Use participial phrases to connect the ideas and reduce the information to one sentence. Check your work by referring to the text above, but there is more than one correct answer.

1 The Company had been interested in remote business models for a long time. Now they are 100% virtual.

2 Millennials are the key to a good staff. This is because they are already accustomed to working remotely.

3 Meetings are now held via video chats. This method is in the process of replacing more traditional types of messaging.

4 Employees tend to work far more efficiently now. A big reason for this is their happiness with their own customized schedules.

C ▶ PAIR WORK Student A: Go to page 157. Student B: Go to page 159. Follow the instructions.

D PLAN You're going to work together to write a profile for one of the companies in exercise 2C. Choose the company and decide what points to include and how to structure your profile. Look at the model in exercise 2A to help you. What points should go in which paragraph?

E PAIR WORK Write a profile for the company you chose.

F GROUP WORK Join another pair of students who profiled a different company. Read your profiles aloud and evaluate each other's work. Then discuss which company you think has the greatest chance of success as a virtual company and why.

TIME TO SPEAK
Make the case

LESSON OBJECTIVE
- prepare and present a case for working remotely

A **RESEARCH** In small groups, look at the key responsibilities of three jobs at Cerben Enterprises, a marketing company with multiple offices in North and South America. Salary and work experience are similar for all jobs.

A
E-marketing manager
- designs email advertising campaigns
- represents Cerben at industry conferences
- manages team of 6–8 employees

B
UX design manager
- responsible for UX on website and internal company site
- tests and improves functionality and features
- leads training sessions for clients and employees

C
Social media manager
- responsible for social media identity
- monitors trends 24/7 and creates content to connect to them
- manages and assigns projects to large freelancer pool

FIND IT

B For each job, brainstorm a list of daily tasks the person in the role is likely to do. You can use your phone to research typical job responsibilities. Discuss which tasks can be done remotely and which can be done better in the office.

e-marketing mgr: write emails – remote   *performance reviews – face to face*

C **PREPARE** The executives at Cerben have decided to allow one of the three jobs above to be based remotely, but which one? Follow the instructions to prepare a case for one of the jobs.

1. Choose one of the jobs. Using your notes from exercise B, consider travel, personnel management, type of work, etc., to build a case for why your job should be based remotely (the pro side).

2. Anticipate counterarguments (the con side) and prepare responses. Prepare at least two good reasons why the other jobs should <u>not</u> be remote.

3. Decide how to structure your points and who will present each part.

D **PRESENT** Present your argument to the Cerben executive team (the class or another small group). Respond to their questions and objections. When you are an executive, refer to the points you prepared against the other roles to pose questions or objections.

E **AGREE** As a class, discuss the arguments and decide which job can go remote. Is there a clear consensus? Is it necessary to vote? How close is the vote? Did any of the jobs get no votes? Why?

 To check your progress, go to page 154.

USEFUL LANGUAGE

PREPARE

Due to the fact that this role is … ,

Anyone working in an office all day knows … , so …

Having read the description for … , I think it's fair to say …

PRESENT

You might think … , but actually …

Thanks to … , the challenges of … are no longer a problem.

The other jobs … . Consequently, ours is the best candidate.

UNIT OBJECTIVES

- discuss shocks and surprises
- talk about great upsets in sports and other contexts
- discuss the differences between local and global brands
- write a paragraph drawing from multiple sources
- prepare a surprise for somebody

START SPEAKING

A   Look at the picture. What emotions is the person expressing? What thoughts might be running through her mind? Through the other person's mind? What would you be thinking?

B   Are you a fan of surprises? Why or why not? What kinds of surprises do you really <u>not</u> like?

C   Would you say that you are a spontaneous person who is open to the unexpected, or do you usually have everything planned? Can you give an example? For ideas, watch João's video.

EXPERT SPEAKER

How similar are you to João?

THE SURPRISE BUSINESS

1 LANGUAGE IN CONTEXT

A **PAIR WORK** Look at the title of the article and the picture. What do you think *Surprise Me!* is? Read the article and check your answers.

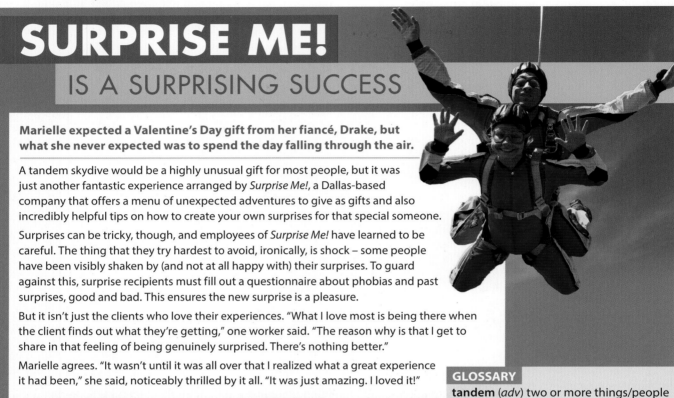

SURPRISE ME!
IS A SURPRISING SUCCESS

Marielle expected a Valentine's Day gift from her fiancé, Drake, but what she never expected was to spend the day falling through the air.

A tandem skydive would be a highly unusual gift for most people, but it was just another fantastic experience arranged by *Surprise Me!*, a Dallas-based company that offers a menu of unexpected adventures to give as gifts and also incredibly helpful tips on how to create your own surprises for that special someone.

Surprises can be tricky, though, and employees of *Surprise Me!* have learned to be careful. The thing that they try hardest to avoid, ironically, is shock – some people have been visibly shaken by (and not at all happy with) their surprises. To guard against this, surprise recipients must fill out a questionnaire about phobias and past surprises, good and bad. This ensures the new surprise is a pleasure.

But it isn't just the clients who love their experiences. "What I love most is being there when the client finds out what they're getting," one worker said. "The reason why is that I get to share in that feeling of being genuinely surprised. There's nothing better."

Marielle agrees. "It wasn't until it was all over that I realized what a great experience it had been," she said, noticeably thrilled by it all. "It was just amazing. I loved it!"

GLOSSARY
tandem (*adv*) two or more things/people acting as one

B **PAIR WORK** **THINK CRITICALLY** Do you think *Surprise Me!* is a good business idea? Why or why not? Would you pay for such a service? How much would you pay?

2 VOCABULARY: Using adverbs to add attitude

A 🔊 **1.47** **PAIR WORK** Read the adverb–adjective phrases in the box. Find five more in the article and write them below. Listen and check. Which adverbs communicate a positive attitude about the adjective? A negative attitude?

deeply (anxious)	immensely (popular)	remarkably (calm)
understandably (upset)	utterly (shocked)	

1 _____highly unusual_____   3 _____   5 _____
2 _____   4 _____

B ▶ Now go to page 146. Do the vocabulary exercises for 6.1.

C **PAIR WORK** Think about something that shocked or surprised you recently. Describe how it felt or your attitude toward it. Combine adverbs and adjectives differently and tell your story.

> My sister and I now go to the same school. She just started here last month, but she is already **remarkably popular**!

3 GRAMMAR: Clefts

A **Read the sentences in the grammar box. Then complete the rules below with words from the box.**

> ### Clefts
>
> **What she never expected was** to spend the day falling through the air.
>
> **What I love most is** being there when the client finds out.
>
> **It wasn't until it was all over that** I realized what a great experience it had been.
>
> **The thing that they try hardest to avoid, ironically, is** shock.
>
> **The reason why is** that I get to share in that feeling.

be	emphasis	it	surprising	thing	what

1 We use cleft sentences for _____ . The cleft is an introductory clause that focuses attention on particularly interesting, relevant, or _____ information.

2 A cleft often starts with the word _____ or the phrase *The* _____ *that* … , but we can also use expressions like *The reason (why)* … or _____ *wasn't until* …

3 Most clefts end with a form of the verb _____ .

B ▶ **Now go to page 134. Look at the grammar chart and do the grammar exercise for 6.1.**

C PAIR WORK **Use the prompts to make sentences that are true for you, and check your accuracy. Share your sentences with a partner and explain your ideas.**

1 The reason [name] loves surprises is …

2 The thing [name] doesn't like about surprises is …

3 How I like to celebrate my birthday is …

4 The surprises that I've enjoyed most were the ones that …

> ✓ **ACCURACY** CHECK
>
> **Don't use *it* between the cleft and the verb *be*.**
>
> *What I love most about my office ~~it~~ is the location.* ✗
>
> *What I love most about my office is the location.* ✓

4 SPEAKING

A ▶ PAIR WORK **Student A: Go to page 157. Student B: Go to page 159. Follow the directions.**

B PAIR WORK **Read the surprises and discuss whether or not each one would be a good choice for the person you read about (Hannah). How might she react?**

> a hands-on visit to a reptile zoo
> an international cooking workshop
> a yoga class on the beach
> an introductory surfing course
> a weekend of whitewater rafting and hiking
> a beginner's photography course

C **Think of a person from your own life who definitely would or would not like each of the surprises above. How do you think they would react?**

> My mother would be **immensely upset** if I took her to a reptile zoo. **The thing she hates most in the world** is snakes!

THE MIRACLE ON ICE

1 LANGUAGE IN CONTEXT

DO YOU BELIEVE IN MIRACLES?

A 🔊 **1.48** [PAIR WORK] **Look at the picture. What sport is this related to? What "miracle" is it talking about? Listen to the radio program and check your answers.**

🔊 **1.48 Audio script**

Today in History
Friday, February 22, 1980: The "Miracle on Ice"

Host   However you look at it, the game still known as the "Miracle on Ice" was one of the greatest sports upsets of all time.

At the Winter Olympics in Lake Placid, New York, Team USA faced the Soviet Union in the ice hockey semifinals. The Soviets had dominated Olympic hockey for decades. By contrast, Team USA was filled with amateurs and college players who had never played together before. In a practice game weeks earlier, the Soviet team's skill and speed utterly overwhelmed the Americans, resulting in a 10 to 3 victory for the Soviets.

Whatever the reason, Team USA was significantly underrated. Fans worried that they might not even score against the Soviet powerhouse. But Team USA shocked the world and beat the Soviet Union 4 to 3.

Sports historian Barry Framm talks about the legacy of this famous upset.

Framm   You know, whenever there's a big upset, it's always compared to the Miracle on Ice – like when an unranked underdog, Roberta Vinci, defeated number one-ranked tennis great Serena Williams in the 2015 U.S. Open.

Host   To find other comparable upsets, you have to leave sports and go into the political arena. Whoever you ask will surely point to Truman's victory over Dewey in the 1948 U.S. presidential election. Overconfident of Dewey's victory, some newspapers actually published front pages with the wrong result!

2 VOCABULARY: Using the prefixes *under-* and *over-*

FIND IT

A 🔊 **1.49** [PAIR WORK] **Look at the words in the box and answer the questions below. Use a dictionary or your phone and the audio script above to help you. Listen and check.**

confident	crowded	developed	estimated	paid
priced	rated	whelmed	worked	

> ❗ For prefixes that are words on their own, like *over* and *under*, there are no definite rules about hyphenation. Choose one dictionary as your reference for consistency in your writing.
>
> ***overwhelmed*** (no hyphen)
> ***over-confident*** OR ***overconfident*** (sources differ)

1 Which of the words can have both the prefix *under-* and *over-*? Which ones typically only use *over-*? <u>Underline</u> the ones that were used in the radio program.

2 Which word is never used *without* a prefix?

3 Find a noun in the audio script that includes one of the prefixes. What do you think it means?

B ▶ **Now go to page 146. Do the vocabulary exercises for 6.2.**

C   PAIR WORK   Replace the underlined expressions with a word that uses *under-* or *over-*, making any changes necessary to the sentence. Which of the statements do you agree with? Why?

1   Some people think professional athletes <u>make too much money</u>. But people <u>don't calculate correctly</u> how difficult an athlete's job is and how unsure their future is.

2   Athletes usually have months off, but during training and the season, they <u>often do more than they should</u>. They sometimes feel <u>unable to handle the stress, physically and psychologically</u>.

3   Of course, some athletes <u>have an ego that is larger than it should be</u>. They would say that they <u>don't get a high enough salary</u>.

3   GRAMMAR: Question words with -ever

A   Read the sentences in the grammar box. Then (circle) the correct options to complete the rules.

Question words with *-ever*
However you look at it, the "Miracle on Ice" was one of the greatest sports upsets of all time. **Whatever** the reason, Team USA was significantly underrated. **Whenever** there's a big upset, it's always compared to the Miracle on Ice. **Whoever** you ask will point to the 1948 U.S. presidential election.

INSIDER ENGLISH

Whatever. = I don't care.
But be careful of your tone of voice!

1   Adding the suffix *-ever* to the question words *who, where, what, which, how,* and *when* indicates that the exact person, place, thing, manner, or time **matters a lot / doesn't matter**.

2   Question words with the suffix *-ever* can also be used to indicate that you **know / don't know** the exact details.

3   Although question words with *-ever* can be found in questions, they **are / are not** used to form questions.

B   ▶ Now go to page 134. Look at the grammar chart and do the grammar exercise for 6.2.

C   PAIR WORK   Use the questions words in the box with *-ever* to make general statements about upsets in sports or politics. Share your statements with a partner. Do you agree with each other?

| however | whatever | whenever | wherever | whichever | whoever |

*Whichever **team** you follow, it is probably going to suffer an **overwhelming upset** at some point.*

4   SPEAKING

A   PAIR WORK   Think about the Miracle on Ice. What other upsets do you know about from different contexts (sports, politics, awards, etc.)?

B   ▶ PAIR WORK   Student A: Go to page 158. Student B: Go to page 160. Follow the instructions.

C   THINK CRITICALLY   Why do people cheer for the underdog? Think of examples to support your opinion. Why might people <u>not</u> cheer for the underdog in a particular situation? For ideas, watch João's video.

EXPERT SPEAKER

In João's example, what would you do?

A SURPRISING COMEBACK

1 LISTENING

A **What do the pictures on this page show? Why might these businesses be seen as surprising?**

B 🔊 **1.50** **LISTEN FOR MAIN POINTS** **Listen to a news feature about the revival of local stores. Circle the two main points the speakers want to make.**

 a Global companies are winning out against local competition.

 b Local stores are making a surprising comeback against big chains.

 c Global business predicted this rise in local independent stores but can do nothing about it.

 d There is a relationship between nostalgia for the past and local independent businesses.

 e Having a store of your own can be surprisingly profitable if you choose the right location.

C 🔊 **1.50** **PAIR WORK** **LISTEN FOR DETAILS** **Listen again and take notes in the chart. Compare with a partner. Did you capture the same information?**

Reasons why local businesses succeed	Reasons why certain things are coming back
People are tired of big chains.	

D **PAIR WORK** **Think of a small business that recently opened where you live. What kind of business is it? Would you say it's part of the trend described in the news feature? Why or why not?**

INSIDER ENGLISH

the good old days = a simpler time in the past

2 PRONUNCIATION: Listening for the pronunciation of foreign words and phrases

A 🔊 **1.51** **Read the sentence and underline the Spanish word. According to English norms, how would you pronounce it? Listen. How does the speaker pronounce it?**

I'm here with Josh Stephens, a longtime resident and a coffee aficionado.

FIND IT

B 🔊 **1.52** **PAIR WORK** **Look at some foreign words and phrases commonly used in English. What language do you think they originally come from? Are any of them also in your language? What do they mean? Use your phone to help you. How do you say them in English? Listen and check.**

avatar	bona fide	cappuccino	carte blanche	chaos	glasnost
hoi polloi	hurricane	ketchup	maelstrom	schadenfreude	tsunami

C **Circle the correct word to complete the sentence.**

When foreign words and phrases are taken into English, they usually *change / keep* their original pronunciation.

3 SPEAKING SKILLS

A 🔊 **1.50** **Complete the phrases for adding emphasis. Listen to the news feature from exercise 1 again to check your answers. Find at least four additional words or phrases for adding emphasis as you listen.**

Adding emphasis

1 Since then, Seattleites have been _____ _____ with the drink.
2 But the _____ that's most surprising is, despite the hundreds …
3 _____ local businesses they want to support now.
4 Vinyl is really making a comeback. _____ new music is coming out on vinyl.
5 Not long ago people really _____ _____ that we'd stop buying books altogether.
6 So, _____, we're talking about two trends here …
7 _____ they have in common is that desire for interaction.
8 I _____ _____ whether this trend … is having an effect on the corporate world.

B **PAIR WORK** **What are some ways to help a local business be successful? Discuss your ideas with a partner. Add emphasis to the points you feel strongly about.**

> What you need is something surprising to make your place memorable. For a record store, you could hire a DJ to play music as people shop.

4 PRONUNCIATION: Saying clefts

A 🔊 **1.53** **Listen to the cleft sentences. Do you hear one or two thought groups? Mark where the intonation goes up and goes down in each sentence.**

1 What the digital revolution has taught us is physical things have value.
2 What they have in common is that desire for interaction.
3 The thing that's most surprising is … small local coffee shops are actually coming back.
4 It is local businesses they want to support now.

B 🔊 **1.54** **PAIR WORK** **Unscramble the words to make cleft sentences. Mark the intonation, and then listen and check. Practice saying the cleft sentences with a partner. Is your intonation appropriate?**

1 really / it / low / costs / was / made / difference / having / the / all / that
2 still / mystery / why / is / the / business / a / failed
3 good / is / the / thing / plan / you / business / a / need

C **PAIR WORK** **THINK CRITICALLY** **Complete the cleft sentences about running a business with your own ideas. Read your sentences to each other. Do you agree?**

1 What I have noticed is …
2 It is your customers that …
3 The reason why most businesses fail is …
4 The thing that separates successful from unsuccessful businesses is …

5 SPEAKING

A **PAIR WORK** **Which types of stores are more successful where you live: multinational chains or local businesses? Why do you think so? Have there been any surprising trends where you live?**

> When McDonald's came to my city, everybody ate there. But that didn't last. People went back to the local sandwich places.

B **GROUP WORK** **THINK CRITICALLY** **What are some advantages that global companies and chain stores have over local businesses? Do you find any of these advantages surprising in any way? If the people in your area had to choose one type or another exclusively, which would they pick? Why?**

JUMP SCARE

1 READING

A Look at the picture on page 61. It's a toy called a Jack-in-the-box. Did you have one as a kid? How does it work? What reaction do people usually have to it? Why do you think kids like it so much?

B **PAIR WORK** **PREDICT CONTENT** Look at the headlines from the collection of texts below. What's the theme of the collection? Explain your ideas.

C **PAIR WORK** **READ FOR MAIN IDEAS** Read the stories and write in the correct headline for each one. Compare your answers with a partner. Discuss any differences in your choices.

An instinct to startle   Sharing the fear   Startled and viral   The simplest "jump scare" ever

 A _____

It takes very little to get Brian Fletcher to jump, and his grandson Mikey loves it! Mikey has quite a following from sharing his "jump scare" videos on YouTube. Watch how Brian leaps out of his seat when a plastic spider falls on his dinner plate or how he jumps halfway across the room when Mikey sneaks up behind his grandfather, peacefully snoozing in his favorite armchair, and blows a whistle. Absolutely everything startles Brian, from a gentle tap on the shoulder to a slamming door. Luckily, he's got a good sense of humor. After each scare, he soon calms down and laughs along with the rest of us!

 B _____

The startle reflex is one of the few instinctual behaviors humans have. Notice what happens when you lay a baby down. They throw out their arms and legs as if to save themselves from falling, but when they feel safe again, they relax. Though it's particularly noticeable in babies, the startle reflex remains part of our biological makeup our whole lives. When we sense danger, it puts the body on full physical alert. For some people, this translates into jumping to their feet. For others, it's a simple tensing of the muscles. Basically, the startle reflex is the first step in the "fight or flight" response of all mammals – that split-second decision of whether to defend yourself or run away.

 C _____

When was the last time you watched a scary movie in a dark theater full of people all on the edge of their seats? With the rise of digital options, movie theaters everywhere are getting smaller or closing completely. Now, most of us just grab the hand of the person next to us on the couch when things get suspenseful. This might be comforting, but it isn't as much fun. Experiencing fear in large groups is enjoyable because reactions are highly contagious. Everybody jumps and screams together. Surprisingly, another very common group response to scary movies is laughter. It's the nervousness that provokes the laughter, then relief when the suspense breaks. Or maybe we just don't want people to know we totally fell for it.

 D _____

On the face of it, it looks like a very simple toy – just a box and a spring and a handle to turn. But this little machine is one of the oldest tricks in the book. No matter how many times you turn the crank, no matter how long it takes for the box to spring open, that moment when the clown pops out still makes your heart skip a beat. You know it's coming, but it still gets you every time! Watch the face of a small child at that fateful moment. Notice how the expression of fear melts almost immediately into a smile of delight. That's the real magic of this toy, not the scare in itself, but the delicious relief of knowing that the danger has passed.

D **TAKE NOTES** Read the texts again. Take notes in your notebook on what the different stories say about each topic below.

the funny side of fear   the exploitation of fear   how humans react to fear

E **THINK CRITICALLY** What fears or phobias do you have? How serious are they? Why do you think we are so fascinated by fear? Why do some people enjoy being scared more than others?

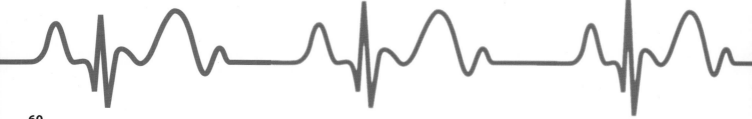

2 WRITING

A   Read this paragraph about one of the topics in exercise 1D. Which topic is it? Which stories in exercise 1C does it draw information from? Does it cover all the information given in the stories?

> **Fear is a basic human emotion. We feel it at all ages.** Even though our reactions can vary in intensity and different events can trigger the reaction, the basic physical response is always the same. Fear can be prompted by relatively simple events. A sudden noise or movement can startle us and set off a chain of physical reactions, even when there is no actual danger. Once the fear has passed, the body relaxes, and we can even laugh at our reaction.

B   PARAPHRASE   Compare the language used in the stories with the language used in the paragraph above. <u>Underline the paraphrases</u> – information from the original text that is stated in different words. <mark>Highlight</mark> the information in the original texts.

 **WRITE IT**

C   PLAN   You're going to write two short paragraphs – one on each of the other topics in exercise 1D. With a partner, follow the steps to prepare:
- Review your notes on the topics in exercise 1D.
- Highlight information in the stories in exercise 1C that relates to each topic.
- Discuss how you could paraphrase the information.
- Review the model paragraph in exercise 2A. How does it start? How does it end? How does the writer paraphrase the information from the stories in the paragraph?

D   Write your two paragraphs. Be sure to include paraphrased information from the stories in exercise 1C.

E   PAIR WORK   Read your first paragraph to your partner. How many of the stories did your partner refer to? Did they paraphrase the information well? Then read your second paragraphs to each other and evaluate them also. Which topic did you each find more difficult to write about? Why?

TIME TO SPEAK
Planning a surprise

A   Look at the picture with a partner. If this was a surprise present for you, what would you hope was inside? What pleasant surprises have you experienced in your life?

B   **RESEARCH**   You are going to plan a pleasant surprise for another pair of students. It doesn't have to be realistic, but it should be something you truly think both of the people would like. Use the topics below and your own ideas to come up with interview questions.

experience of past surprises
fears / phobias / allergies
interests / hobbies / abilities
response to being startled or scared
"wish list" ideas (places they want to go to, etc.)

C   **DECIDE**   Interview the other pair. Discuss their responses and come up with a plan. Write notes for yourself about the key elements and why you chose them. Use the example to help you.

> Surprise for Pavel and Manny: A diving vacation in Madeira
>
> Madeira: P loves scuba, M wants to learn
>   famous for diving; lots of diving schools
>   M spks Portuguese
>   Nice weather all year
>
> 2-BR apt: P likes to cook (can't in hotel)
>   M can bring wife (also wants to learn to scuba)
>
> 5 days: both have busy jobs

D   **PRESENT**   Tell the class about the surprise you planned. Be sure to reference the other pair's responses to explain your choices. Let the intended recipients ask questions to clarify points. Then ask them to give your plan a rating from 1 (not a good plan) to 10 (excellent plan).

E   **AGREE**   As a class, review which pairs got the highest ratings on their surprise plans from the intended recipients. What did they do that the lower-rated pairs didn't do? If you could pick whatever surprise you wanted for yourself, which one would you choose? Why?

To check your progress, go to page 154.

USEFUL PHRASES

RESEARCH

We should ask if they prefer …
A good question would be, "How do you feel about … ?"
Let's be sure to ask about …

PRESENT

The reason why we chose X is because …
The best thing about this surprise is …
They can … whenever they want.

REVIEW 2 (UNITS 4–6)

1 VOCABULARY

A **Complete the paragraph with the correct words.**

abandoned impact anonymous elaborate mammoth source filthy eye to eye blind motivated

I've worked as a freelancer for years. Like everything, there are pros and cons, but working from home has had a positive ¹_____ on my health. I used to work in an open office with hundreds of people in it. The atmosphere felt so ²_____ , like nobody even knew who you were or what you did. It didn't help that I never saw ³_____ with my boss, either. I didn't like him, and he didn't like me. My coworkers came in late and left early all the time, and he just turned a ⁴_____ eye to it. But if I was five minutes late, he yelled at me.

Now, I'm my own boss. No more ⁵_____ , complicated management structure. Just me. No more ⁶_____ room full of unhappy people. Just a comfortable little office next to the living room. And it's clean, too – the bathrooms at my old office were ⁷_____ . At first, I worried that I might feel lonely, ⁸_____ , isolated. But then I realized that a big ⁹_____ of stress at my old job was other people. Working alone is great, and it has ¹⁰_____ me to do more things socially, which is also great. I should have quit that awful job years earlier!

B **PAIR WORK** **Discuss other advantages of working from home. What disadvantages can you think of?**

2 GRAMMAR

A **Use the words in parentheses ( ) to combine the sentences into one.**

1 I have a lot of nice coworkers. I've known many of them for quite a while. (whom)

2 I do lots of different tasks at work. Different skills are required for every task. (each)

3 I receive a lot of emails. I don't even read most of them. (the majority)

4 I used to work in restaurants. As a result, I know what goes on in those kitchens! (Having)

5 I live alone. The last thing I want to do is work alone, too. (Living)

6 I was excited to see my name in the paper. I didn't even notice that it was misspelled. (So excited)

B **PAIR WORK** **Look at the sentences in exercise 2A again. Which are true for you or somebody you know? Share your stories.**

3 VOCABULARY

A (Circle) the correct words to complete the story.

I have to tell you this story about the day I got lost. We were in a remote place in the Amazon. I was
¹*genuinely surprised / visibly shaken* when the guides told me our route because it didn't seem to be
the usual path. But I was an experienced hiker, though perhaps a little ²*overworked / overconfident*.
The landscape was beautiful and ³*barren / lush*, but it was hard to see under the trees. These two factors
⁴*resulted in / motivated* me getting separated from the group. Also, I had ⁵*overestimated / underestimated*
how quickly it gets dark in the jungle. But I have to say I stayed ⁶*utterly upset / remarkably calm*. I was
sure the group would soon realize I wasn't with them and come find me.

One day later, I was still alone. By then I had become ⁷*understandably anxious / noticeably shocked*: I was
lost in this ⁸*vast / picturesque* jungle, and I was starting to believe that nobody would ever find me.
Just as the sun was starting to go down, I heard voices. It was the search party! The feeling of relief was
⁹*overwhelming / overrated*, and I was so happy to see them I couldn't speak. My rescuers were so nice and
¹⁰*visibly unusual / immensely helpful*. They gave me a blanket and food and water, and they made me
feel safe and secure immediately.

B PAIR WORK **Has anyone you know ever gotten lost in a remote place? How did they feel? How did
it all turn out?**

4 GRAMMAR

A **Complete the sentences with an appropriate word or phrase from the box. More than one answer
may be possible.**

however	the reason	the thing	what	whatever	wherever

1 _____ I never expected was <u>to speak English so well</u>.
2 _____ you live, <u>English is an important language</u>.
3 _____ I like about my hometown is <u>people are so friendly</u>.
4 Say _____ you want about <u>politicians</u>, but <u>I just don't trust them</u>.
5 _____ I'd like to <u>live abroad</u> is <u>that it would widen my horizons</u>.
6 _____ <u>expensive</u> it is, <u>traveling is worth it</u>.

B PAIR WORK **Do you agree with the statements above? Why or why not? Change the <u>underlined</u> parts
and make new statements with your own ideas.**

GRAMMAR REFERENCE AND PRACTICE

1.1 COMMENTING ADVERBS WITH FUTURE FORMS (PAGE 3)

Using commenting adverbs with future forms

Commenting adverbs with future forms express the speaker's opinion or attitude about the likelihood or desirability of an action or condition. They generally follow the modal *will* or the verb *be* in future expressions.

1 *will* + commenting adverb + (*not / never*) + verb OR commenting adverb + negative contraction (*won't*, *aren't*, *shouldn't*) + verb

   They **will undoubtedly become** part of everyday life.

   They **probably won't gain** a lot of support among labor unions.

2 future expressions

   ■ *be* + commenting adverb + *going to* + verb: the action is planned or intended

   ■ *be* + commenting adverb + *about to* + verb: the action will happen very soon

   ■ *be* + commenting adverb + *bound to* + verb: the action cannot be avoided

   This **is inevitably going to cause** problems.

   It **is undoubtedly about to change** everything we do.

   They **are definitely bound to be met** with resistance.

A **Put the commenting adverb in parentheses ( ) in the correct position.**

1 Robotic nurses will become a fixture in all modern hospitals. (inevitably)

2 They are going to take over most of the heavy lifting work from nurses. (undoubtedly)

3 There are bound to be a few problems as medical staff get used to working with a machine. (certainly)

4 They are about to change hospital practices forever. (surely)

1.2 FUTURE PERFECT AND FUTURE CONTINUOUS (PAGE 5)

Future perfect and future continuous

Use the future perfect and the future continuous to describe situations in the future.

1 *will* + *have* + past participle (the future perfect): For actions that will be completed by a point in the future or before another event in the future

   Chatbots **will have taken over** from humans by the end of the next decade.

   Will they **have taken over** on helplines, too?

   They **won't have taken over** on all helplines.

2 *will* + *be* + verb + *-ing* (future continuous): For actions that will be, or are planned to be, in progress at a given time in the future

   We**'ll be having** real conversations with them.

   Will we **be having** real conversations with them?

   We **won't be having** conversations with real people anymore.

A **Circle the correct form of the verbs to complete the sentences.**

1 If my train's on time, I'll *be knocking / have knocked* on your door at ten o'clock sharp.

2 By the end of the semester, we will *be covering / have covered* most of the material in the book.

3 By this time tomorrow, we'll *be flying / have flown* to Hawaii for a two-week vacation!

4 We'll *be meeting / have met* with the head of Research and Development at the conference next week.

5 I hope I'll *be having / have had* time to read the book before we meet to discuss it.

2.1 USES OF *WILL* (PAGE 13)

Uses of *will*

The modal *will* can be used in many different situations:

1   To make predictions, assumptions, and deductions about the future
    *Online personality quizzes **will** always **give** positive, flattering results.*
    *In five years, we **will** all **be seeing** much more targeted advertising.*
    *By the time you read this, you'**ll have seen** hundreds of quizzes on social media.*

2   To describe typical behavior, habits, and things that are true now or in general
    *Personality quizzes **won't** ever **provide** truly valuable information.*

3   To express decisions about the future made at the point of speaking
    *I **will** never **take** another personality quiz! This one was totally wrong.*

4   To criticize habits, behavior, and characteristics   *Quiz developers **won't admit** to their real motivation.*

5   For making offers, agreeing, and promising   *Our site **won't** ever **misuse** or **sell** personal information.*

A   **Use the information given to write sentences reflecting the different uses of *will*. Which use does each of your sentences relate to?**

1   My grandmother loves to bake. She has always offered to make cakes for special occasions in our family.
    My grandmother loves to bake. She'll always offer to make a cake for a special occasion.

2   Don't bother asking Sylvester to help you. He says no to everything.

3   My father loves to talk about politics, but he told me that he wouldn't do that when my girlfriend's parents come over for dinner next week.

4   You've worked in this building for a year. Do you know that the elevator isn't very reliable? Of course you do.

5   I answered a call from an unknown number, which was just a robocall trying to sell me something. Now I get calls like that all the time. Never again!

2.2 USES OF *WOULD* (PAGE 15)

Uses of *would*

The auxiliary verb *would* is used in many different ways:

1   To refer to past habits and typical, expected behavior   *When I was a kid, I **would ride** my bike everywhere.*

2   To make polite requests   ***Would** you **help** me with these bags, please?*

3   To express an opinion or judgment politely   *I **would think** he'd wear something nicer to a wedding!*

4   To report a statement or question with *will*   *He promised I **would get** the job.*

5   To express what someone or something is willing or able to do   *The car **wouldn't start**, so I had to walk.*

6   To talk about actions in an unreal situation   *What **would** you **do** in that situation?*

A   **Rewrite the sentences using *would*. Which use does each of your sentences relate to?**

1   Close the door.

2   That seems like a perfect job for you. What's the problem?

3   He said he was going to arrive at eight.

4   That's so typical of him to say that.

5   In those days, I used to walk for miles.

6   I asked him many times, but he didn't say anything.

3.1 VARIATIONS ON PAST UNREAL CONDITIONALS (PAGE 23)

Variations on past unreal conditionals

Different conditional constructions can be used to talk about past unreal situations. Continuous forms express actions in progress, in both the *if* clause and the main clause. The *if* clause can come first or last in a sentence.

1 To express a situation where both the unreal condition (*if* clause) and the imagined result are in the past, use:
   - *if* + *had*(*n't*) + past participle | *would*(*n't*) + *have* + past participle
     *If you'd told me, I **would have written** it down.*
   - *if* + *had*(*n't*) + *been* + verb + *-ing* | *would*(*n't*) + *have* + past participle
     *We **would've missed** the announcement if you **hadn't been paying** attention.*

2 To express a situation where the unreal condition is in the past, and the imagined result is in the present, use:
   - *if* + *had*(*n't*) + past participle | *would*(*n't*) + verb
     *If you **hadn't heard** the announcement, we **would** still **be** at the station.*
   - *if* + *had*(*n't*) + past participle | *would*(*n't*) + *be* + verb + *-ing*
     *If you **hadn't heard** the announcement, we **would be waiting** on the wrong platform now.*
   - *if* + *had*(*n't*) + *been* + verb + *-ing* | *would*(*n't*) + verb
     *If you **had been watching** the children, Oliver **wouldn't have** a broken arm now.*
   - *if* + *had*(*n't*) + *been* + verb + *-ing* | *would*(*n't*) + *be* + verb + *-ing*
     *If you **had been watching** the children, we **wouldn't be cleaning** up this mess now.*

A   Write the correct form of the verbs in parentheses () to complete the sentences.

1   If he _____ (pay) attention, he _____ (notice) that the chair was broken.

2   If you _____ (wait) as long as I have, you _____ (complain), too.

3   This _____ (not happen) if you _____ (watch) what you were doing.

4   You _____ (enjoy) the party more if you _____ (wear) a costume like the rest of us.

5   I _____ (still sit) on the side of the road if he _____ (not help) me change my flat tire.

3.2 COMMENTING ON THE PAST (PAGE 25)

Commenting on the past

Use the modal verbs *may*, *might*, and *could* to discuss possible alternative scenarios. Use *should* and *shouldn't* to criticize actions or lack of action. Use perfect forms after the modals when commenting on the past.

1 For a completed action, use *may/might/could* or *should* + *have* + past participle.
   *She **may/might not have heard** the full story.*

2 For an action in progress, use *may/might/could* or *should* + *have* + *been* + verb + *-ing*.
   *You **could have been telling** a story about someone else.*

3 For passive voice, use *may/might/could* or *should* + *have* + *been* + past participle.
   *That information **shouldn't have been shared** with the public.*

A   Complete the sentences with *should* or *shouldn't* and the appropriate form of the verb in parentheses ( ). Use the progressive form where possible.

I'm really sorry. I really ¹ _____ (check) before taking the keys. I ² _____ (pay) more attention, but I was distracted. But you know, you ³ _____ (not leave) your car keys out in the first place.

I ⁴ _____ (not leave) the bike outside, and I ⁵ _____ (use) a lock. I was in a big hurry, but I know I ⁶ _____ (rush). I ⁷ _____ (give) myself enough time. But even so, the bike ⁸ _____ (not steal) at all. I can't help it if bad people steal things!

4.1 QUANTIFIERS AND PREPOSITIONS IN RELATIVE CLAUSES (PAGE 35)

Quantifiers and prepositions in relative clauses

To add details in a relative clause, use quantifiers such as *all of, each of, many of, most of, much of, none of, some of*.

1   Use *which* for things and *whom* for people. (When used with a quantifier, *which* cannot be replaced by *that*.) To avoid confusion, place the relative clause immediately after the person or thing it refers to.
*Microphotography gives a fresh perspective on everyday <u>objects</u>, **most of <u>which</u> we usually ignore**.*
*<u>Microphotographers</u>, **many of <u>whom</u> are scientists**, focus on the tiniest details.*

2   In speech and in most written registers, prepositions in relative clauses come after the verb. In formal or academic writing, you will often see the ending preposition before the relative pronoun.
*Special microscopes, **which cameras are attached <u>to</u>**, bring out the delicate details of pollen and dust.*
*Special microscopes, **<u>to</u> which cameras are attached**, clarify the structure of the pollen molecule.*

A   **Combine the sentences using relative clauses. Use quantifiers where appropriate. Be sure prepositions are correctly placed for an informal context.**
1   I took hundreds of photos on my vacation. Most of my pictures are really awful.
2   We've invited about a hundred people to the party. Many of these guests will have to stay at a hotel.
3   My mother and I both told you about a great book I was reading. It's now available in paperback.
4   I'm working at a restaurant right now. That man over there is the manager of it.
5   This old book is full of words that are very strange to me. I had to look up many of the words.

4.2 NOUN CLAUSES WITH QUESTION WORDS (PAGE 37)

Noun clauses with question words

1   Question words can replace general nouns in noun clauses:
   - *what* = the thing / things
   - *who* = the person / the people
   - *why* = the reason
   - *how* = the way
   - *where* = the place / location / the point in a process or story

   *I didn't know **why** you wanted to see me.*
   ***How** eyes adjust to light levels is by expanding or contracting the pupil.*

2   Noun clauses with question words can be the subject or object of the verb.
   Subject: ***What we see** is a world of grays.*
   Object/complement: *Iris scanning proves we are **who we say we are**.*

3   Noun clauses with question words use statement word order. They are <u>not</u> questions.
   *I can't remember **where <u>I left</u> my glasses**. (<u>not</u> where ~~did I leave~~ my glasses.)*

A   **Replace the bold words with the correct question word.**
1   This is **the reason** I love summer. _____
2   Spending time with my family is **the thing** I like to do more than anything. _____
3   I love **the way** you talk to the kids in your class. _____
4   If I know **the location** you're standing, I can find you on GPS. _____
5   **The way** we see the world is an important part of **the people** we are. _____ _____
6   The man in the hat is not **the person** the police are looking for. _____
7   You need to pay more attention to **the things** your grandfather tells you. _____
8   I can play most of the song, but the chorus is **the point at which** I always have trouble. I don't know **the reason**.
   _____ _____

5.1 PARTICIPLE PHRASES IN INITIAL POSITION (PAGE 45)

Participle phrases in initial position

Participle phrases at the beginning of a sentence add extra information about the main action or the subject of the sentence. They are often used to avoid repetition and to shorten complex sentences. A participle phrase <u>doesn't</u> contain a subject.

1   Begin with a present participle to describe an action in progress at the same time as the action in the main clause.
    Feeling overwhelmed by the crowd, he quickly made his way to the exit.

2   Begin with *Having* + past participle to describe an action that happened before the action in the main clause.
    Having experienced the beauty of a desert sunset, she became determined to move to Arizona.

3   Begin with a past participle to describe the subject of the sentence (in the main clause).
    Convinced this was his last chance, John dropped everything and ran to catch the train.

Participle phrases in initial position sound formal and are more common in writing than in speech.

A   **Rewrite these sentences using participle phrases. Which of these sentences are true for you?**

1   After I finished college, I took a year off to travel.

2   Because I live on my own, I mainly eat out.

3   I was totally exhausted after a hard week, so I decided to take it easy on the weekend.

4   I didn't have a lot of time today, so I took a taxi here.

5   I was so relieved that I passed all my exams. I had a big party to celebrate.

6   I have almost finished my English course. I'd like to learn another language now.

5.2 REDUCED RELATIVE CLAUSES (PAGE 47)

Reduced relative clauses

A relative clause contains a relative pronoun (*which, who, that*) and a verb phrase. When the verb of the relative clause is *be* and there is no subject pronoun, the clause can be reduced by dropping the relative pronoun and *be*.

1   *be* + verb + *-ing*   Tourists ~~who are staying~~ on the island need to book their hotel room early.

2   *be* + adjective   Students ~~who are interested in~~ visiting the sites need to sign up at the office.

3   *be* + past participle   Areas of the site ~~that are surrounded~~ by fences cannot be visited by the public.

4   *be* + prepositional phrase   Requests ~~which are from approved organizations~~ will be given priority.

A   **Rewrite the sentences using a reduced relative clause.**

1   I've just read a great book that is entitled *Ancient Aztecs*.

2   I thought the man who was walking down the street was my neighbor, but I was wrong.

3   She will be on the train, which is arriving on platform 3.

4   I know a lot of people who are worried about their health.

5   Students who are concerned about climate change should join the environmental action group.

6   People who are familiar with her work say that this piece is one of her best.

7   Buildings that are older than 100 years can be submitted to the Preservation Society for consideration.

8   Conditions that are well suited to one species may not be conditions that another even closely related species could survive in.

6.1 CLEFTS (PAGE 55)

Clefts

Clefts are introductory clauses that are used to emphasize new information or something particularly interesting or surprising. Clefts can take several forms:

1   *What … + be*   **What she wanted was** *a big party!*
2   *The thing (that) … + be*   **The only thing we wanted to do was** *dance!*
3   *The … (that) … + be*   **The only guests at the party will be** *people from school.*
4   *It + be + that/who/when*   **It was my uncle** *who told me the good news.*
     It wasn't until they brought out a cake *that I realized the party was for me!*

A   **Use the words in parentheses ( ) to rewrite the sentences with clefts. More than one correct answer is possible.**

1   Some people don't like surprises because they make them feel embarrassed. (thing)

2   My mom loves surprises because life is usually so predictable. (reason)

3   A surprise was on its way, but he didn't know that until he read the card. (it)

4   I really miss the birthday surprises I had when I was a kid. (what)

5   I'd really like to go to the Galapagos Islands on our honeymoon. (place)

6   While we're there, we really hope to see John's cousins. (people).

6.2 QUESTION WORDS WITH *-EVER* (PAGE 57)

Question words with *-ever*

Question words can be changed to pronouns by adding the suffix *-ever* (*whatever, whichever, whenever, wherever, whoever, however,* but rarely *whyever*). They indicate uncertainty or indifference (<u>not</u> a question):

1   To indicate that nothing will change the result
     Whatever *the critics say, I think it's a great movie.*   *We'll get there,* ***however*** *long it takes.*
2   To indicate that the other person is free to choose   *Sleep* ***wherever*** *you like. There are lots of free rooms.*
3   To indicate that the details are uncertain or unimportant   ***Whoever*** *told you that was lying. It's not true.*
4   To indicate that the speaker doesn't mind, doesn't care, or has no opinion.   **A** *When should we arrive?*
     B ***Whenever****. People can come and go as they like.*

A   **Add the appropriate question word with *-ever*.**

1   _____ good their campaign was, I don't think they'll win the election.
2   He says he'd like to get together, but _____ I try to set something up, he says he's busy.
3   _____ you want to go for dinner is fine with me. I'll eat anything!
4   _____ we do to help, they always complain.
5   I'm voting for Sarafina, but I'll help _____ wins. It's too big a job for one person.

VOCABULARY PRACTICE

1.1 USING ADVERBS TO ADD DETAIL (PAGE 2)

A **Write the appropriate adverb using the word in parentheses ( ). What do you think the development might be?**

1 This is _____ (question) one of the greatest developments in public transportation in the last ten years!

2 It will _____ (radical) change the way we move around our cities and _____ (drastic) cut back on our consumption of fossil fuels.

3 It will _____ (progress) take over for all traditional modes of transportation.

4 People could _____ (feasible) save time and money, as well as help the environment.

B **Circle the correct adverbs to complete the paragraph.**

Introducing the new robot surgeon, the radical medical development that is ¹*drastically / gradually* being introduced in hospitals around the world. Currently, the robots are directed by a human and can only perform a limited range of operations. The hope is, however, that they will ²*increasingly / unquestionably* be able to perform all kinds of major surgery. Researchers expect robot surgeons will ³*markedly / ultimately* reduce surgical errors, possibly by as much as 25 percent. The robots will ⁴*inevitably / progressively* meet with resistance from patients, but they will soon see how effective robot surgeons can be.

1.2 TALKING ABOUT DEVELOPMENTS IN TECHNOLOGY (PAGE 4)

A **Complete the sentences with the correct form of an appropriate word or phrase from the box.**

artificial intelligence (AI)	beta version	computer-generated speech	chatbot
computer translation	facial recognition	image recognition	
operating system (OS)	text to speech / speech to text	virtual assistant	
voice activation	voice recognition	working prototype	

1 Recent developments in _____ mean that computers are getting better and better at imitating human thought.

2 This new home-security software uses _____ technology, so your front door won't open until it hears you say it's OK.

3 I can't open any of these work files on my laptop at home. I think my office computer must use a different _____ .

4 There have been stories in the news recently about _____ that seem to be laughing at their owners and are refusing to answer their questions!

5 The researchers are currently trying to get a _____ of their robot ready to show investors. If they get enough funding, they could have a beta version in a year.

B PAIR WORK **Read the needs and decide which type(s) of technology would address them best. Then write four needs and think of the best ways to address them. Compare your work. Can you think of other technology that might address your partner's needs?**

1 You need to identify an object in a photo.

2 Passport machines need to check passenger identity.

3 You need to run programs on your computer.

4 A digital help line needs to answer simple requests for information.

5 You want to dictate a message on your cell phone.

6 You need to check your email, but you're driving.

7 An app company needs to test their new product and find "bugs."

8 A message on a social media feed is in Korean, but you want to read it in English.

9 _____

10 _____

11 _____

12 _____

2.1 DESCRIBING PERSONALITY (PAGE 12)

A Complete the sentences with the words in the box.

accepting	chatty	genuine	insensitive	rigid	self-centered

1 I like that he's so _____ and sociable, but he has to learn to shut up sometimes.
2 My parents are very _____. I wish they could relax a little and be a bit more flexible.
3 I thought that question was very _____. I understand why they were offended.
4 Teenagers tend to be pretty _____. But they grow out of that and start caring about the rest of the world eventually.
5 I think she'll be a good therapist because she's very _____ and not at all judgmental.
6 When you're a little child, you're _____ and honest. You don't hide your feelings at all.

B (Circle) the correct adjectives for the context of the paragraph.

My roommate Selma is amazingly sweet. I've never heard her say a negative thing about anyone! There's this guy in our building who never says hello. I think he's ¹*antisocial / genuine* and unfriendly, but Selma tells me not to be ²*narrow-minded / sincere*. He's just shy. But there's no reason for him to be so ³*aloof / talkative*. I may be a little ⁴*open-minded / talkative* at times, but "hello" isn't much to expect. Selma says I'm a ⁵*rigid / sincere* person who likes to connect with others, which is why it bothers me. I think that's her nice way of saying I'm kind of pushy.

2.2 USING THREE-WORD PHRASAL VERBS (PAGE 14)

A Complete the sentences with correct form of the phrasal verbs in the box.

come down to	fit in with	get through to	mess around with	stand up for

1 It's really hard to _____ him. He has such rigid ideas and doesn't want to listen.
2 I thought he was serious about working this weekend, but he was just _____ me.
3 I owe her a big favor because she _____ me when nobody else would.
4 He has good ideas for new products, but they don't really _____ the rest of the product line. I think he should start his own company.
5 I don't care about fancy brands and fashion. For me, it all _____ comfort.

B Match the two parts to create collocations. Then use the collocations in context in the sentences below.

1 fall back on ____   a people
2 face up to ____   b any nonsense
3 look down on ____   c opposition
4 run up against ____   d established ideas
5 not put up with ____   e (their) mistake

1 They _____ who don't dress well. I don't like their superior attitude.
2 The bosses at my company are so afraid of taking risks. They always _____ and never want to try anything new.
3 I wish Mariella ran these meetings. She _____, and we'd surely finish more quickly.
4 We all wanted her for the job, but we _____ from headquarters when they saw that she doesn't have a college degree.
5 My son and his friends broke a window at school when they were messing around. They could have run away, but they _____ and reported it. They even paid for the repairs.

3.1 THOUGHT PROCESSES (PAGE 22)

A **Write the words in the box next to their definitions.**

analyze	disregard	fixate	foresee	presume	review

1 a be obsessed with a
   particular idea _____
  b think that you know _____
  c be able to predict the future _____

  d think something is not important _____
  e look back over something _____
  f examine something in detail
    in order to understand it _____

dismiss	envision	evaluate	interpret	reconsider	reject

2 a change your point of view _____
  b decide something is not
    worth considering _____
  c imagine a future situation _____

  d don't accept something
    because it isn't good enough _____
  e explain what something means _____
  f consider the value of something _____

B (Circle) **the word that is different from the others.**

1 analyze   evaluate   interpret   reconsider
2 disregard   dismiss   fixate   reject
3 envision   foresee   interpret   predict

3.2 DESCRIBING EMOTIONAL REACTIONS (PAGE 24)

A **Complete the sentences with words from the box.**

flustered	gracious	harmless	mellow	resourceful	spiteful	victorious

1 After that truck nearly hit us, I was so _____ that I had to pull over and calm down for a while.

2 John has a very particular way he likes to mow the lawn. It's _____ , so I don't try to stop him. Who cares how he does it as long as he does it?

3 With no money for decorations for the play, we had to be _____ . We used green paper for the bushes and made flowers from balloons!

4 When our team's design was chosen for the campaign, we walked around feeling _____ for weeks!

5 His coworker was so angry about Pablo's promotion that he started doing little things just to cause problems. His behavior was really childish and _____ .

6 During the presentation, I completely forgot to give Sharon credit for her work. I felt awful, but she was really _____ about it. She said everyone makes mistakes when they're nervous.

7 Big parties are OK, but I usually prefer a more _____ gathering, like a small dinner party.

B (Circle) **the correct adjectives to complete the paragraph.**

What's the most important thing a manager should always remember?

"Don't take it personally."

When people are looking to you for answers, it can feel like they're questioning your judgment, which can easily make you feel [1]*defensive / victorious* about your decisions. Just remember, it's not about you. The workplace can be tense and stressful, which can cause people to blow things out of proportion and become [2]*harmless / hysterical* over the smallest problem. If you stay calm and [3]*composed / resourceful*, people will follow your lead. If you're [4]*melodramatic / spiteful*, you'll only add to their anxiety. But nobody's perfect. If you do lose control, admit it and apologize. People are [5]*flustered / forgiving* when they believe you're sincere.

4.1 DESCRIBING THINGS (PAGE 34)

A **Which adjectives from the box would you use to describe the things? More than one correct answer is possible. Compare your answers with a partner.**

circular	cylindrical	delicate	elaborate	filthy	flaky
mammoth	miniature	multicolored	ridged	stringy	

1 your favorite dessert
2 your favorite athlete's uniform
3 your favorite musical instrument
4 an animal you can see in a zoo
5 a piece of jewelry that you like
6 a machine you have in your home

7 decorations related to your favorite holiday
8 a space ship (real or from a movie)
9 a mountain in your country
10 equipment in a doctor's office
11 the design on the rug or curtains in your room
12 the oldest book you ever saw

B **PAIR WORK** **Think of common objects from daily life and take turns describing them to your partner using the adjectives in exercise A and others. Don't use your hands when you talk. Can your partner guess the object from your description?**

4.2 EYE IDIOMS AND METAPHORS (PAGE 36)

A **Match the expressions to their definitions.**

1 agree   i
2 be aware of everything around you
3 ignore (usually something bad)
4 focus on your main aim
5 enjoy looking at
6 draw your attention unexpectedly
7 not caring about the result
8 seeing something from above
9 very quickly
10 currently well-known and in the media
11 using imagination

a a bird's eye view
b catch your eye
c feast your eyes on
d have eyes in the back of your head
e in the blink of an eye
f in the public eye
g in your mind's eye
h keep your eyes on the prize
i see eye to eye on
j turn a blind eye to
k without batting an eye

B **Replace the bold words with idioms and metaphors from exercise A.**

see eye to eye on
1 I don't need to ~~share opinions on~~ absolutely everything to be friends with someone.

2 If you know that someone is doing something wrong and you **don't do anything about** it, you're just as guilty.

3 This map doesn't give any details. It just gives **a wide-angled perspective** of the area.

4 Long-term goals are more difficult than short-term ones. But no matter what obstacles come up, just **remind yourself how wonderful it's going to be when you've finished**, and you'll get there.

5 Most celebrities prefer that their kids not be **the subject of media attention**, so they have to be careful not to take them places where there's paparazzi.

6 We waited forever for the check. Finally, I managed to **get** the server's **attention** and ask for the bill.

7 Never take your attention off the road when you're driving. An accident could happen **very quickly**.

8 **Get a good look at and enjoy** our showroom full of beautifully restored sports cars from the 1970s!

5.1 DESCRIBING REMOTE PLACES (PAGE 44)

A (Circle) the correct words to complete the sentences. Which sentences are true for you?

1 I love landscapes that are vast and *barren / picturesque* – great empty lands like Patagonia or Iceland.

2 I don't feel comfortable in *deserted / nameless* places, especially if there are lots of *abandoned / anonymous* buildings around.

3 My favorite landscapes are rich, green places that are *hostile / lush*, with different types of vegetation.

4 I like to hike through the forest to a scenic overlook spot on top of the mountain. It has a beautiful view of the *barren / immense* landscape that goes on for hundreds of kilometers!

5 There is a *harsh / vast* area in the center of my country where there aren't many people, only forests and plains. Most people live near the coast.

B **For each group, match the words in the box to their synonyms.**

anonymous	harsh	immense

1 a very large   _____
   b difficult to
      live in   _____
   c unremarkable   _____

abundant	isolated	scenic

3 a plentiful   _____
   b by itself and hard
      to reach   _____
   c pleasant to look at _____

abandoned	hostile	picturesque

2 a empty   _____
   b visually attractive _____
   c uninviting   _____

barren	lush	unspoiled

4 a not touched by people _____
   b with few living things _____
   c rich and abundant   _____

5.2 TALKING ABOUT INFLUENCES (PAGE 46)

A **Rewrite the ideas in the sentences using words from the box. More than one answer is possible. Compare sentences with a partner.**

consequence	force	impact	implications	influence
motivate	result in	source	stem from	trigger

1 The accountant noticed some unusual items in an expense report and asked the owner of the company about them. Soon, a full investigation of company finances happened.

2 After the government announced it was closing the local school, parents were worried about how this would affect their children's lives.

3 Sometimes a big problem causes you to think about things differently. This can lead to a really surprising or interesting way to solve the problem.

4 Many adult problems exist because of experiences that happened in childhood.

5 When they try to explain their own work, musicians often refer to the music or styles of other musicians that they like or admire.

6 Many factors shape the final design of a product, for example, money, time, target market, and the creativity of the design team.

B PAIR WORK **Discuss the questions.**

1 What (not who) has had the greatest positive influence on your life? What aspects of your life has it impacted?

2 What forces motivate people to make big changes in their lives? Have any of these forces triggered action in you?

3 Imagine you were offered a great job in a country far away. What implications would taking the job have on your family? Your friends? Your current employer?

6.1 USINGS ADVERBS TO ADD ATTITUDE (PAGE 54)

A **Choose an appropriate adverb–adjective combination to complete the sentences. More than one correct answer is possible.**

Adverbs	deeply	genuinely	highly	immensely	incredibly	noticeably	remarkably	utterly
Adjectives	anxious	calm	helpful	popular	shocked	surprised	thrilled	unusual

1 When they announced that they were getting married, I was _____ _____ . I didn't even know they were dating!

2 That play was _____ _____ . I've never seen anything like it before.

3 It was a tense situation, but she remained _____ _____ throughout.

4 The guy at reception was _____ _____ and gave us lots of useful tips.

5 I could tell that Max was _____ _____ . He kept jumping up and down in excitement.

6 That movie has been _____ _____ . There are still lines down the block to get tickets.

7 I was _____ _____ when they made me an offer. I didn't think the interview went very well at all.

8 He's been _____ _____ these last few days. He still hasn't heard whether his company is going to get the contract. His business really needs the work.

B **PAIR WORK** **Use the prompts to talk about your experiences. Add attitude with adverbs when you can.**

1 Something that was immensely popular but you didn't like: Why?

2 An experience that made you noticeably anxious: What happened?

3 A time when you were remarkably calm while others were not: What happened?

4 Behavior that utterly shocked you: Why?

5 A product you are highly surprised to find is genuinely helpful: What is it? What does it do? What did you expect?

6.2 USING THE PREFIXES *UNDER-* AND *OVER-* (PAGE 56)

A **Add *under-* or *over-* to the words in the box to match the definitions. More than one correct answer may be possible.**

confident	~~crowded~~	developed	estimated	paid	priced	rated	whelmed

1 too many people   *overcrowded*

2 receiving wages that are too low for the job _____

3 too expensive for what it is _____

4 feeling too sure about a result _____

5 not calculated high enough _____

6 not able to handle something because it is too much _____

7 without modern facilities _____

8 reviewed as lower than it should be _____

B **Rewrite the ideas in the sentences using *over-/under-* words.**

1 The critics gave this movie five stars, but I didn't like it at all.

     I think this movie is overrated. It got five stars, but I didn't like it!

2 Even if you think you're perfect for a job, prepare well for the interview. You never know what will happen.

3 I think this phone is a real bargain. People would pay twice as much for it!

4 If you're claustrophobic, don't take the subway between 5 and 7 p.m. There are a lot of people trying to get home after work at that time.

5 In the U.S., servers in restaurants don't have high salaries, so they depend on tips to get by.

6 I have too much work to do this month! It's really stressful.

PROGRESS CHECK

Can you do these things? Check (✓) what you can do. Then write your answers in your notebook.

Now I can …

☐ use commenting adverbs to express an opinion.

☐ use commenting adverbs to talk about future probability.

☐ talk about changes in technology.

☐ use future perfect and future continuous to describe future actions.

☐ acknowledge arguments and propose counterarguments.

☐ write an essay about future possibilities.

Prove it

Use four adverbs from the unit to discuss how useful robots could be in your community.

Write three predictions related to technology using commenting adverbs.

Use four words from the unit to describe a tech item, its functions, and what it is used for.

Write about a future machine and how it will have changed life and what we will be doing differently because of it.

Respond to this argument with two different counterarguments: "Robots will eventually take over the service industry."

Look at your essay from lesson 1.4. Find three ways to make it better.

Now I can …

☐ describe someone's personality.

☐ use *will* to talk about assumptions, deductions, and predictions.

☐ talk about labels and their effects on people.

☐ use *would* in a variety of contexts.

☐ compare and discuss similar experiences.

☐ write a report based on graphs.

Prove it

Use adjectives to describe the personality of someone you know well.

Rewrite the sentence using *will*: They always share their quiz results with friends and are not likely to stop.

Write sentences using these phrasal verbs: *look down on, fit in with, get through to, stand up for, put up with.*

Rewrite the sentence using *would*: I'm not willing to make assumptions about someone based on their age.

Write two ways to say you had the same experience as someone and two to say you understand their feelings.

Look at your paragraphs from lesson 2.4. Find three ways to make them better.

Now I can …

☐ discuss ways to think about past actions and their effects on the present.

☐ react to past situations.

☐ describe emotional reactions.

☐ comment on the past.

☐ describe a negative experience and offer sympathy and reassurance.

☐ write a short story based on a set of facts.

Prove it

Describe a past situation that you regret. What happened? Describe the thought processes that led you to change your mind.

Write three sentences about your hindsight situation proposing different actions and results. Use *if* constructions.

Describe a past situation in which you reacted emotionally. What happened?

Respond to the situations using the prompts:
"I ran out of gas." (should / pay attention)
"I can't find my passport." (could / leave)

Write three different ways of showing sympathy and offering reassurance to somebody who has had a bad experience.

Look at your story from lesson 3.4. Find three ways to emphasize the coincidences more.

PROGRESS CHECK

Can you do these things? Check (✓) what you can do. Then write your answers in your notebook.

UNIT 4

Now I can …	Prove it
☐ describe things.	Describe something in your home but not in the classroom to a partner. Can they guess what it is? Take turns and describe five things.
☐ use quantifiers and prepositions in relative clauses.	Write four sentences about eyes using quantifiers and prepositions in relative clauses. For example, "My cousins, *all of whom* have their father's green eyes, also have their mother's dark skin."
☐ talk about how eyes function.	Write three expressions about eyes in context.
☐ use question words in noun clauses.	Use your expressions in sentences with question words. For example, "We have never seen eye to eye, so in planning meetings *what we mostly do* is argue."
☐ use expressions to clarify points or highlight problems.	Think of an issue with different viewpoints. Write three sentences clarifying your own perspective. For example, "The *truth of the matter is* …"
☐ write a personal statement for a résumé.	Look at your profile statement from lesson 4.4. Find three ways to make it better.

UNIT 5

Now I can …	Prove it
☐ describe remote places and landscapes.	Think of two very different remote landscapes you have seen pictures of. Use adjectives to describe them.
☐ use participle phrases in initial position.	Write four sentences about the above landscapes using initial participle phrases. For example, "*Looking at the lush forest*, I …"
☐ talk about influences and how they have affected your life.	Choose three things that have influenced your life choices and describe them. Then think of three personal habits and think of possible reasons for them.
☐ use reduced relative clauses.	Combine sentences you've written above using reduced relative clauses. For example, "Anyone afraid of snakes should not travel there."
☐ discuss the pros and cons of working from home.	Write two responses to signal a cause and an effect. 1 Working from home is gaining popularity. 2 Some remote workers feel lonely.
☐ write a company profile.	Look at your company profile from lesson 5.4. Find three ways to make it better.

UNIT 6

Now I can …	Prove it
☐ discuss different reactions to unexpected events.	Write five adverb–adjective combinations. Use one of them to talk about something that surprised you recently.
☐ use clefts to make sentences more emphatic.	Write three things that you like and give reasons why using clefts. Use *reason, thing, it,* and *what* one time each.
☐ use words with the prefixes *under-* and *over-* to modify descriptions.	Give your opinion on six things that you think are not fair or accurate in some way. For example, "I think most pro athletes are *overpaid* because …"
☐ use questions words with -*ever* to show uncertainty or indifference.	Write four questions and responses with question words with -*ever*. For example, "What time should we leave?" "*Whenever* you want."
☐ add emphasis in different ways in a discussion.	Write one example sentence for each emphasis technique: Adverb–adjective combination, cleft, adverbial (*even, at all*, etc.), auxiliary *do*.
☐ write a paragraph drawing from multiple sources.	Look at your paragraphs from lesson 6.4. Find three ways to make them better.

PAIR WORK PRACTICE (STUDENT A)

3.4 EXERCISE 2C STUDENT A

FACTS:

- Two people with the same name turn up at a hotel.
- Both made reservations on the same day at the same time but on different booking sites.
- They live in different cities, but their street addresses are the same.
- There's only one room booked under the name.

5.4 EXERCISE 2C STUDENT A

1 **Read about two companies.**

Company A: Educational publisher

This company decided to create online products only and avoid traditional paper-bound books. Only executives and marketing staff work in-house, but there are teams of freelance workers who produce the digital content and design it using online platforms. Freelance project managers oversee the whole process.

Company C: Expat retailer

This company sells typically American products, everything from food to clothes, to Westerners living in Hong Kong and Singapore. They decided to close their brick-and-mortar locations and operate online only. Their payroll (money paid to employees) has been cut drastically, but shipping costs have increased greatly.

2 **Choose one of the two stories and summarize the information for your partner.**

6.1 EXERCISE 4A STUDENT A

A **Read a post on a social media group for fathers and take notes.**

So most of you know my youngest daughter, Hannah, graduated from high school last week, and that I'd been struggling to come up with a way to celebrate other than the usual, boring graduation party. She had a difficult year and worked really hard, so I wanted to do something incredibly special for her. But what? She loves traveling and learning languages. And she's always been a very adventurous eater – she'll try almost anything, especially seafood – so I thought about getting her a trip abroad somewhere on the coast. But then, I thought "No, that's been done. I want to do something *really* different." And I wanted it to be something she'd never expect but would remember for the rest of her life.

Well, I'm happy to say, I totally nailed it! We just got back from the trip of a lifetime to Arches National Park in southern Utah. I'd never been, but some coworkers had told me about it, and it sounded like the perfect surprise for Hannah. It was just amazing. If you've never been, you have to go. It's just this remarkably beautiful desert landscape with bare, red rock formations. I've never seen anything like it. And the wildlife! We saw little desert foxes and bighorn sheep. Coming from the city, it was just awe-inspiring.

But the best part was that she didn't expect a thing! I told her to pack her bag for the airport, but I didn't tell her where we were going. You wouldn't believe how surprised she looked when she figured out where we were headed! Seriously: Best. Trip. Ever.

B **Share key information from the post with your partner. Then do exercise 4B on page 55.**

PAIR WORK PRACTICE

6.2 EXERCISE 4B   STUDENT A

1 **Read about another famous upset.**

Crash wins Best Picture Oscar against all odds.

Crash won the Best Picture Oscar at the 78th Academy Awards in 2006, controversially beating the critically favored *Brokeback Mountain*. A thriller set in LA, *Crash* was only the second film ever to win the Best Picture Oscar without being nominated for any Golden Globe Awards. Many felt that *Crash* won because some judges were uncomfortable with the subject matter presented in *Brokeback Mountain*. Even *Crash* director Paul Haggis said in a 2015 interview that he did not believe that his film deserved to win Best Picture. In this case, the underdog was not the popular favorite.

2 **Tell your partner about the story. What do your two stories have in common? Which one do you think is more surprising? Why?**

3 **What factors might have contributed to this situation? Were people overconfident that *Brokeback Mountain* would win, or was *Crash* perhaps underrated?**

PAIR WORK PRACTICE (STUDENT B)

3.4 EXERCISE 2C   STUDENT B

FACTS:

- A woman lost a ring on the beach.
- Six months later, she finds the ring in a secondhand shop 200 kilometers away.
- The woman in the shop was on vacation at the same beach at the same time.

5.4 EXERCISE 2C   STUDENT B

1 **Read about two companies.**

Company B: Architecture firm

This company closed its office, and employees now work remotely. They meet regularly online to discuss current and future projects. Without an office, employees must travel to their clients and bring along whatever is needed. For this reason, any new employee or freelancer must live near where their projects are based.

Company D: Food delivery cooperative

The small restaurants on one street joined together to centralize their delivery services. Instead of each restaurant taking orders and delivering, all orders go through one app. The restaurants split the costs evenly, regardless of which restaurant gets the most orders day by day. They had to hire a few employees to manage the service, but they need a lot fewer freelance delivery people.

2 **Choose one of the two companies and summarize the information for your partner.**

6.1 EXERCISE 4A   STUDENT B

A **Read Hannah's email to her friend and take notes.**

Soooooo… I just got back from that surprise graduation trip with my dad and… I don't even know where to start. Seriously, WHAT is wrong with him? He told me to pack a bag for a four-day trip, but he wouldn't tell me where we were going. Since I'd been studying Spanish, I figured maybe we were taking a trip to Mexico – Cancun or Playa del Carmen or some other beautiful coastal town. He knows I've always wanted to go to those places. And a week just relaxing on the beach? Yes, please!

Anyway, we get to the departure gate at the airport and they announce, "Now boarding for the 8:30 flight to Salt Lake City, Utah." My dad's like, "Surprise! We're going camping in Arches National Park." Camping… in the desert. I packed a swimsuit and flip-flops! I tried to look excited, but I think my dad could tell I was annoyed.

Things just got better and better once we got to Utah. ☻ The first day, I almost stepped on a rattlesnake. I'll bet you could have heard me screaming from halfway across the park. And that night I could hear wolves – actual wolves – howling outside our tent.

I mean, don't get me wrong, it was beautiful. And, yes, it was really great to spend some quality time with my dad. But it was my graduation trip… I just wish I'd had a chance to take a shower!

B **Share key information from the email with your partner. Then do exercise 4B on page 55.**

PAIR WORK PRACTICE

6.2 EXERCISE 4B   STUDENT B

1   **Read about another famous upset.**

Uruguay beats Brazil in the 1950 World Cup against all odds.

The 1950 World Cup tournament was held in Rio. In the final match, the Brazil team just needed a draw to secure its first trophy. Brazil had outscored opponents 21 to 4 in their previous five matches and had beaten Uruguay 5 to 1 in the previous year's South American championship, leaving Brazilian media and fans certain they would win. But underdog Uruguay utterly shocked the crowd by beating their host 2 to 1. In this case, almost nobody was cheering for the underdog.

The match became known as the *Maracanazo* (*Maracanaço* in Portuguese), after Maracanã stadium where the match was played. The "Phantom of '50" lives on in Brazil's collective imagination, and each time the two countries play, the story is retold.

2   **Tell your partner about the story. What do your two stories have in common? Which one do you think is more surprising? Why?**

3   **What factors might have contributed to this situation? Was one team underestimated or overrated, for example?**